A. F. Bourns.

E. Thomson

OUR

ORIENTAL MISSIONS.

VOLUME I.

INDIA AND CHINA.

BY

EDWARD THOMSON, D. D., LL. D.,

Late Bishop of the Methodist Episcopal Church.

CINCINNATI:
HITCHCOCK AND WALDEN.
NEW YORK:
CARLTON AND LANAHAN.
1870.

PREFACE.

THE following pages are substantially a Journal kept by the writer during a visit to the missions of the Methodist Episcopal Church in the years 1864–65. It was not with the intention of publishing it that the Journal was written, but with a view to make out a full report to the Church in case it should be called for. Brethren, in whose judgment the narrator confides, have latterly urged him to give it to the public, and as it cost him but little pains to revise it, he yielded to their opinion. In the revision he has modified here and there an observation, and put reflections in a new form, but has made no material alteration. Our missions in the East are, it is hoped, destined to become very important, and the time may come when their history shall be written. Perhaps this volume may furnish some dates and materials for such a history. It will certainly serve as a mile-stone to mark progress. Scarcely four years have elapsed since these pages were written, and yet the intensely interesting letters of Bishop Kingsley, which the reader has most assuredly read, and which ought to be given in book form without delay, will show a marked advance, not only in the progress of religion in the East, but in the condition of the world. Now one can circumnavigate the globe with much more ease and safety than he could in 1864; and, go where he will, he will find society advancing, and in the great centers where the Christian religion is permeating the minds of men. It is a matter of profound regret that the Methodist Episcopal Church has not done more for her missions than she has. The Centenary, the vast field opened at home, and the results of the war will naturally be referred to as accounting for our want of enlargement abroad, but we must not plead any excuses hereafter. Let us look forward, not backward. If this book shall in any measure contribute to awaken the interest of the Church in our foreign missions the writer will have no occasion to regret its publication.

It is hoped the reader will not read with a critical eye. One on a journey can not write carefully; and he who knows what is required of a preacher in the relation in which the writer stands must know that he can give no time to authorship. He has attempted nothing but a plain statement and the natural reflections thereon.

E. T.

EVANSTON, ILL., *March*, 1870.

CONTENTS.

Our Oriental Missions.

I.

FROM NEW YORK TO CEYLON.

I EMBARKED at New York on the 24th of August, 1864, was safely borne across the Atlantic in the Persia, and landed at Liverpool on the 4th of September. Here I preached in one of the oldest churches of the Wesleyan connection, and within the walls of which the British Conference authorized Dr. Coke to go out on his mission to Ceylon; a mission which he was not allowed to plant, as he died on the outward passage to the East. From Liverpool I proceeded to London, and preached at Lambeth Wesleyan Chapel. Engaging passage by the Messageries Imperiales I was soon on my way to Marseilles. Embarking here on board the steamer "Peluse," I had a pleasant passage across the

Mediterranean, touching at Messina, and debarking at Alexandria.

From Alexandria we are hurried by railway to Cairo. Here we have an opportunity to see something of the capital of Egypt, its citadel, its celebrated mosques, the Nile, and those colossal monuments of ancient art, the Pyramids. From Cairo we are conveyed by railway through an unbroken desert, under a burning sun, seeing nothing but here and there a railway station, and off in the distance a caravan of camels, until we reach Suez. This is a small, miserable-looking place, with unpaved streets, and houses of undried brick, deriving all its importance from its being a port on the overland route to the East, and the terminus of the canal recently opened for small craft, which connects the Red Sea and the Mediterranean. It contains, however, a good hotel for the accommodation of European travelers, a narrow bazaar, and a few shops for the sale of European goods. It stands near the head of the Gulf of Suez, and not far from where the Israelites crossed on their exodus from the land of bondage. While the sun was setting, and the Muezzin was calling the faithful to prayers, we embarked on a lighter along-side the quay, and were soon off for the roadstead two or three miles distant, where the "Tigre" rode at anchor, ready to receive us on our route to the distant East.

Shortly after sunrise on the following day we set sail for Calcutta. When we were barely under way two sailors, standing on a plank, fell into the sea. One, in falling, caught a rope, the other, while floating, a life-preserver, and, after a time, both were safe upon deck, though one was very much exhausted. The Red Sea is of dangerous navigation, in consequence of its numerous coral reefs and concealed rocks; and its passage is uncomfortable by reason of its excessive heat. The temperature of the air is seldom below 80° Fahrenheit at any season of the year. The temperature of the water is as high, and, sometimes, even higher. In November, 1856, when the air was 82° Fahrenheit the water was 106° Fahrenheit. The wind is S. S. E. from October to June, and N. N. W. from June to October. Sailing down in September we had but little wind; just about enough to cancel the breeze created by the passage of the vessel, and produce a perfect calm. Most of the time the air was at 92°, the water nearly the same. Many of the passengers slept on deck, but as the amusements were sometimes protracted till late in the evening, and the washing of the decks commenced at 4 o'clock in the morning, their slumbers were short, unless they took a supplementary sleep after descending to their berths. Another objection to sleeping on deck arises from the heavy dews of the night. There is but little rain here, and the evaporation from the surface amounts to eight feet annually. Many perish, in their passage down this sea, from the excessive heat. I suffered very much myself, and though I took a bath every morning it did not afford me much relief.

Our first stop is at Aden, in Arabia. It is on an arid spot at the foot of rugged rocks, which, but for the tower, would present a picture of perfect barrenness and desolation. It derives its importance from being a coaling station for ships on the way to India, and a fort from which the British Lion can keep guard over the path to its most important colonial possession. Here are a few stores, a tavern, a post-office, and a multitude of laborers, some Arabs and some Somanlies and Abyssinians. You can here obtain a glass of water for a few cents, which, however, will hardly bear examination with the microscope, or even with the naked eye, and reminds us of the saying that water is a good thing for navigation, and machinery, and washing, but a poor thing to drink. A mile or two distant is a military station, where is a regiment of soldiers, a bazaar, and a series of spacious tanks, made at immense cost, for receiving and preserving the rain which now and then falls down the mountain's side. The coolies here go nearly naked, and are very skillful in diving for silver coin which travelers sometimes throw into the water to test their abilities. Before we left the Gulf we passed within sight of the mountain range to which Sinai belongs, though we did not see the venerated summit from which the law was given. After leaving the Gulf of Suez we see but little of the shore, but wherever we do catch a glimpse of it it is mountainous.

Leaving Aden we are soon in the Straits of Babelmandeb. This is divided into two channels by the Island of Perim. We take the little strait, which is between the island and the Arabian shore. Perim is a black and barren rock, without water and almost without vegetation, but as it contains a good harbor, and commands the entrance to the Red Sea, the British have taken possession of it, and fortified and garrisoned it. They had no right to do so except the right of the strong, but they were induced to exercise this in consequence of the construction of the Suez Canal by the French. We are soon out of the straits, coasting along the Island of Socotra, whose bold shores, lofty mountains, and beautiful green surface afford a pleasant relief to the eye wearied with the sea, and remind us of the date, the aloes, and the dragon's blood. And now we are fairly in the Indian Ocean; the breezes become cooler, and, except where we have a touch of the Simoon, the company feel their exhilarating influence, so that music and dancing may be heard far into the night.

This company is nearly all European—mostly English—some in the military service, some in the civil; some capitalists, and some merchants; some alone, but many with their wives and daughters. Among the number are wives and children returning to their homes, and maidens going to their betrothed—who are in danger of losing their hearts on the way. All for wealth! but, alas! what a terrible tax to pay for it! A man, in the East, must reconcile himself either to raise a family under heathen influences, or be separated from them during their period of pupilage. He must see his wife fade away prematurely, or send her to the hills, or to the West. No *money* could compensate me for such privations. If, however, men can endure them for the sake of gain, shall we not for the sake of Christ? It is pity that they who go from Christian lands do not carry better principles, move with purer motives, and set a better example. As a general rule Christians, who go to the East to make money, never get their religion through the Straits of Gibraltar. There is more known on that subject than it is profitable to relate. No wonder the heathen are so slow to receive the Christian religion. They consider that eating pork and drinking brandy are its characteristic attributes. They are, however, now beginning to distinguish between a nominal and a real Christian. In India they denominate the first a *cutcha* Christian, the other a *pucca* one. A new road opened through the woods is *cutcha;* a metaled or turnpiked one is *pucca*; a house made of mud is a cutcha one; a house built of stone and brick, and covered with cement, is a pucca one.

The emigration to the East differs, in one respect, from that to our own country. The Western people go to Asia, not as colonists, but as traders. They leave their homes behind them, and look backward longing. They can never, therefore, feel that interest in the country, nor in its inhabitants, that they should. Indeed, the climate is too hot for them, and they entertain a prejudice against the dark races that belong to it as strong as we have ever indulged toward the African slaves. This is particularly true of the British. The Portuguese, Spanish, and Dutch have much less of this prejudice, and in their colonies marriages not unfrequently occur between them and Asiatics. The Eurasians in *English* possessions are generally illegitimate, and often despised by both races; and even where they are the issue of lawful matrimony both they and their parents are, to a great extent, excluded from the society alike of natives and of foreigners.

At Ceylon, we land at Point de Galle; a good harbor on the southern side of the island. On entering the tavern we heard of the terrible cyclone of October 5th. The cyclone is a fearful storm. It is expected in the Fall with greater or less severity every year, and it seems to recur with excessive violence about once in ten years. Thus it appeared with terrible force in 1833, then in 1842, again in 1852, lastly, in 1864. It travels in a circle; that of 1864 was seventy miles in diameter, and its course was traceable for two hundred miles. We, who live in this latitude, can form no just idea of such a storm. The ships that on the morning of the 5th of October lined the bank of the Hooghly in tiers of three to four deep, from Fort Point to Armenian Ghat, a distance of two miles, one hundred and ninety in all, had before night either broken from their moorings, and been tossed at the mercy of winds and waves, or had ground against each other until they had sunk at their anchorage. The strand road, which runs along the river bank, six feet above high-water mark, was, for two miles, strewn with shattered fragments of boats, fallen trees, railings, etc. The opposite shore was lined with masses of ships mingled in inextricable confusion, while the bodies of men and animals by thousands floated by. The barometer at one time sank to 28.50, and the pressure of the gale varied from five to thirty-two pounds per square foot. At Koogoree the storm-wave reached the height of twenty-five to thirty feet above high-water level; sweeping whole villages away, carrying ships into the jungle, and leaving them high and dry among the trees. One steamer was carried inland farther than a telegraph station, and others were cast into gardens, on the tops of piers, and on the public roads. Had the water risen six feet higher the whole city of Calcutta would have been submerged.

The following is an official list of the casualties in the city of Calcutta:

Natives killed, ...	41
Natives wounded, ...	12
Pucca houses damaged, ...	1,383
Pucca houses destroyed, ...	18
Cutcha houses destroyed, ...	89,412
Europeans killed, ...	2
Europeans wounded, ...	5
European houses damaged, ...	2,296
European houses destroyed, ...	92

The loss of life from Saugor island up to Calcutta is estimated at two thousand men, women, and children. After the storm, in many cases, the mails for the country were returned, because the villages to which they were sent were not found.

The island of Ceylon is of great beauty. You ride between hedges of luxuriant flowers, among which are the Leuria, or American Currant, and roses of great variety, and beneath the grand foliage of the bread-fruit-tree, the jack-tree, and the cocoa-nut palm, and you inhale delicious fragrance, sometimes of the cinnamon, the clove, and the temple-tree, whose blossom is like a white tulip, and whose odor is surpassing. The people are a sluggish, dark-colored race, of but little information, and little industry. The coolies, or laborers, at the port and in the interior are generally nearly naked, and they wear their hair as women do here; done up behind with a tortoise-shell comb. They are very numerous; living in villages overshadowed by their luxurious woods, which are said to contain four hundred and thirteen varieties of trees. Of these the cocoa-nut palm is the most valuable. The large leaves furnish fences for the garden; the smaller leaves, (plaited,) roofs for the houses; the flower stalks, torches; the nutshell, household utensils; the fibrous covering, ropes, matting, and nets; the sap, arrack; the fruit, when green, both food and drink, and when dry a most valuable oil. Each tree rents for about five shillings a year. Rice, cotton, tobacco, coffee, pepper, and cinnamon are important productions of the island.

The northern part of the island is inhabited by Tamils, the southern by Singhalese—people different in their origin and characteristics. The language of the first belongs to the Scythian family, that of the second to the Sanscrit. It was in Ceylon that I first made myself acquainted with paganism. The temples are generally located in high, picturesque situations, and surrounded by pleasant grounds, which belong to them. Near the temple is a pagoda, in which the priests profess to keep relics and valuable offerings. The images of Buddha are colossal, and represent him either as sleeping, preaching, or meditating. The usual offerings of the people are flowers. Near the temple is a court, in which, on certain days, the people assemble to hear a harangue from the priests; and, usually, in the rear of this court is the dwelling of the priests. With these are to be found some boys and young men in training for the priesthood. The priests are celibates and mendicants, and are arrayed in yellow robes. Some of them go out from each temple once a day to receive the offerings of the people, spice, rice, etc. They are, however, allowed to enter into busy life, and marry, if they choose; and if they get tired of domestic life they can divorce themselves and return to the priesthood. The priests received me very kindly, and at every temple presented me with an orange or some other little present. There is one among them of much learning and distinction. He has established a printing-press, and is issuing a series of tracts, derived from the works of Colenso and other English infidels, against the Christian religion. He recently visited the King of Siam, who, to favor his project, gave him a handsome subscription. He was polite to us, inquired about our war, and expressed great pleasure at seeing an American clergyman.

Devil worship, which once prevailed all over India, was the original religion of Ceylon, and for thousands of years held the people in thralldom. Nor has it ceased. Indeed, from what I saw, I had reason to believe that it has far more power over the people now than Buddhism. When they are sick they send for the demon priests; and the doctors encourage this when they have a difficult case. These priests are shrewd men, who follow their business to make money. They are fantastically dressed, go in companies, and entering the house dancing and making noises, and going through ceremonies which one would suppose must either kill or cure the patient. Sometimes they pretend to trick the devil by going through the ceremony of burial, and then invoking the devil to leave the house, because the patient is gone.

Polyandria once prevailed among this people, and although the government has laudably endeavored to break it up, it still obtains in some regions. It is found very economical for several men to join in supporting one wife, one enjoying her society one week, another another week; or, one having her one-seventh, another, two-sevenths, and a third four-sevenths of the time, according to the amount they respectively contribute to the support of the household. Economical as the arrangement may be, it does not strike us as very good. With us, love is an *exclusive* affection. If we love a woman we do not want any body else to love her, and should not like any partnership in regard to our households. But, if a rich man may have as many wives as he can support, why may not a poor woman have as many husbands as are necessary to support her? Pleasantry on this serious subject aside, we see how necessary the Christian religion is to regulate the social relations of mankind. In 1630 the Portuguese conquered the island, but the court of Lisbon overlooked both the duties and the privileges which the conquest imposed, and its agents did more to gratify their lust of power and of money than to civilize the natives and develop the resources of the island. In 1658 the Dutch drove out the Portuguese. The new-comers were rather merchants than statesmen. They sought, however, to convert the natives to the Protestant faith, though by means unsuitable. They enforced attendance at school by fine; administered baptism and solemnized marriages in the schools; making the schoolmaster keep a register of these events. They forbade any one to hold office or farm-land under government who had not been baptized in the Protestant Church. To extinguish the Catholic faith, introduced by the Portuguese, they declared Roman Catholics ineligible to office, and, while conferring freedom on all children born of Protestant parents, doomed the children of Catholics to perpetual slavery. The result was that the people became hypocritical, and many lowland chiefs and aspiring priests came forward for baptism while secretly clinging to the symbols and the principles of heathenism. The influence of this policy is still seen in the desire of the people to be baptized, if they can without renouncing heathenism. In 1796, during a war between England and Holland, the British conquered Ceylon, and they have held it ever since. Their rule has been good; they have opened roads, established schools, improved cultivation, extinguished slavery, introduced law, and, above all, through the various missionary societies, spread abroad the Christian faith.

It was my privilege to visit several missions and mission schools, and I can bear testimony to the fidelity of the missionaries, and the excellence of their institutions. I examined classes in English Grammar, Geography, Biblical History, and Chronology, and found them well prepared. Among the questions was this: "What prophecies of the Messiah are contained in the Old Testament, and how have they been fulfilled?" On Sabbath I preached in the Old Dutch Reformed church, to a congregation composed chiefly of descendants of the early Dutch settlers. Many of these are Eurasians. But, though dark-colored, they speak European languages, and have European dress and manners. In the evening I preached for the Wesleyans, who are, to a considerable extent, composed of a similar society.

II.

VOYAGE TO CALCUTTA.

AN opium steamer having been sent down to convey us to Calcutta, we set sail for that port, stopping at Pondicherry and Madras. On the way we encountered the cyclone of the 21st of October. Our ship, however, outrode the storm, though driven from her course. On our way we met with many vessels damaged, and when we reached the Hooghly we began to see the terrible effects of the first cyclone. At one place we saw the wreck of a vessel in which three hundred coolies went down to a watery grave. The ship was literally inverted. At another point we saw the Bentinck, a ship of the largest class, high up on the shore, and when we reached Calcutta we beheld a city that looked as if it had been shelled by an enemy. It was evening as we drew near the port, and we beheld on the banks of the stream for the first time the fires of the funeral pile. It was to me a strange and melancholy light. Fearing to damage the shipping in port, we anchored below Garden Reach all night, and slipped up early in the morning of the next day.

Eastward of Alexandria we meet with no wharf. At Pondicherry, at Madras, is only an open roadstead, and here we anchor in the stream, and go ashore in a dingy, a small, narrow, native boat. Reaching Calcutta we take a ghary for the Spencer House, a large, airy, lofty tavern, built in the Oriental style. After breakfast we take our first ride in the palanquin. It is no pleasant conveyance, and I soon exchanged it for a ghary, in which I visited the Asiatic Society's Museum, the Geological Museum, the Public Library, the Agricultural Museum, the Baptist missions, the Wesleyan missionaries, etc. I was not long in Calcutta before I had the pleasure of meeting Rev. Dr. Butler, who came down from our mission field to accompany me up. Calcutta has been called the city of palaces. Like all Indian cities, it has a black town and a white town ; the former for natives, the latter for Europeans. The one has narrow, unpaved streets, and mud or bamboo houses, the other has spacious avenues, high brick buildings, covered with stucco, and ornamented with verandas. The strand is a fine drive along the river bank. The public edifices are spacious and elegant, especially the Bishop's College, the Cathedral of St. Paul, and the Government House. Fort William lifts up ramparts which require 600 cannon, and 9,000 men to man them. Garden Reach is a beautiful suburb, with country seats and elegant gardens. Among them is the residence of the late king of Oude, who, with a royal salary, is always in debt; and no wonder, for they say he has one hundred wives.

The population is between 600,000 and 700,000, of which 10,000 are Europeans. The mean temperature is 66 degrees Fahrenheit in January, 69 degrees in February, 80 degrees in March, 85 degrees in April and May, 83 degrees in June, 81 degrees in July, 82 degrees in August and September, 79 degrees in October, 74 degrees in November, 66 degrees in December. The hot season begins in April, and the heat increases till June, when the thermometer is often 100 and 110 degrees. Numerous public monuments adorn the city, commemorative of Gen. Ochterlony and Lords Hardinge, Bentinck, Auckland, and others distinguished in the Indian service. Then there is a Burmese Pagoda in Eden Gardens, which, when I saw it, was pretty well demolished by the cyclone. At Messina, in Sicily, there came on board a young Brahmin, who had been to

England to complete his education, and who, having passed a competitive examination, had received a commission in the Indian civil service. He was a youth of fine abilities and most amiable character, and I formed a very intimate acquaintance with him. He is a son of Baboo Tagore, of Calcutta, a Zemindar of great wealth and influence, and who is the founder of the Brahmo Somaj, an organization of Deists which is becoming an important element in the moral forces of India. The society was established more than twenty-five years ago. Beginning in a sort of Vedic philosophy, which recognized the infallibility of the Vedas and the sanctity of the Brahmins, and "blew the sacred couch, and rang the sacred bell," it has at length reached a simple theism. It at first took external nature as its teacher of religious truth, but finding that insufficient, it has learned to depend on the *internal* light, or religious consciousness. Its members study the works of Colenso, Newman, Theodore Parker, and other English and American skeptics. The writings of Thomas Paine are to be found translated in India, but the Brahmos are too cultivated to be pleased with his blasphemy. It professes to be Catholic and Eclectic; recognizing some truth in all forms of faith, and selecting from Western and Eastern religions those principles which it approves, crying with Emerson,

> "I am owner of the sphere,
> Of the seven stars, and the solar year;
> Of Cæsar's hand, and Plato's brain;
> Of Lord Christ's heart, and Shakspeare's strain."

It differs from the Deism of the West in two important particulars. It maintains a devotional spirit; assumes an organic form; it has a Church, a liturgy, and a sort of priesthood; it gathers in its converts, and sends out its agents to preach alike against Hindooism, Mohammedism, and Christianity; it is thoroughly iconoclastic, and, so far as it is destructive, it is useful; but it presents no definite faith, and exercises no moral discipline over its members. Its mode of operating upon the nation is peculiar. Regarding Hindooism as the representation of the national character, and desiring to preserve the national life, it would adopt the national religion and modify it, or, rather, adapt the new religion to Indian Sociology, Philosophy, and modes of action, so as to preserve the Hindoo character and the whole machinery of Hindoo society complete. Its ideas are, however, unsettled. At first it deemed God too merciful to punish, now it deems him too just to forgive. The day after I reached Calcutta young

Mr. Tagore called upon me to say that in consequence of damage done by the cyclone to the church of the Brahmos, the next meeting of that body would be in his father's chapel, and that they would be happy to see me there. Accordingly, at the appointed time, I set out for it in company with Dr. Butler. We found, in passing through the native city, an intolerable smoke, and were assured that it is always experienced in the evening, and results from the fires of the natives, who do their cooking at this period; often in fire-places without chimneys, and filled with cow-dung, which is the chief combustible of the country.

The house of the Baboo is high and substantial, and built round a spacious court. In the first story, extending across one side, is the chapel; a beautiful apartment, capable of accommodating three or four hundred worshipers, with a pulpit and orchestra. Every thing about it is tasteful and Grecian. Behind the pulpit were numerous inscriptions in Sanscrit, Hindoo, Arabic, Persian, etc.; such as, "God is one, and there is no second," "God is true," "God is good," "God is beautiful." The worshipers were all men, chiefly young, and dressed in white robes. They sat upon the marble floor during the whole service. Mr. Tagore and two other gentlemen seated themselves in the pulpit, and the worship commenced. It consisted in reading select passages from the Shasters, prayers, chants, and hymns—with instrumental accompaniment—and excogitations from the breast of Mr. Tagore, etc. The assembly was orderly, and, apparently, devout. Many of them moved their bodies backward and forward; a motion in which they seemed to have imitated those who occupied the pulpit. At our entrance we were seated in two arm-chairs that were provided for us. After service the younger Baboo invited us to tea. Besides himself, his brother and the chief lecturer of the association appeared at the table, but none of the rest of the family. The lecturer is a well-educated and accomplished gentleman. He goes to the different cities of India to declaim against idolatry, and organize affiliated societies. The meeting produced mingled feelings of joy and sorrow, hope and fear.

It is easy to understand how young men, educated in the government schools of India, lose faith in their own religion, and, as they have no better presented to them, lose faith in all. It is easy, too, to perceive how this institution, at present simply theistic, will become otherwise. The utterances of Baboo Tagore are taken down and printed, and they already constitute a book.

This book will soon come to be regarded as inspired, since its sentences are supposed to come from the inner monitor, or divine guide.

From Calcutta we proceed by railway to Benares, through Serampore, the seat of the first Baptist mission in India, Shandernagore, Burdwan, Dinapore, Patua, and Buxar. The distance is 540 miles. We crossed the Ganges on a bridge of boats. It was night when we arrived. The city, lighted up, made a fine appearance from the stream. Here we were met by Mr. Sherring and Mr. Blake, of the London Missionary Society, and kindly taken to the house of the former. One can hardly enter such a place as this without emotion. Benares is regarded by the Hindoos as coeval with the birth of Hindooism, and is a place of holiness and heavenly beauty. It calls forth the same longing as the Mohammedan feels to visit Mecca, and, hence, attracts crowds of pilgrims. It was here that, in the year 588 B. C., Sakya Muni, the last and only historical Buddh, on attaining Buddahood, first "turned the wheel of the Law" in the monastery, now known as Sarnath; a position which he sought as one from which he could best influence the nation. Benares must, therefore, have been regarded as the ecclesiastical capital of the country at that early period. The Hindoos have a foolish tradition that it existed before the Flood, and that Mahades balanced it on his trident, and thus saved it from the waters. It is, however, but a sober opinion that Benares was flourishing while Athens was but beginning, and, perhaps, may have furnished Solomon with gold to adorn the Temple. Macaulay's famous description in his "Warren Hastings" is still correct, only that he puts the population too high. He says it is "a city which, in wealth, population, dignity, and sanctity was among the foremost of Asia. It was commonly believed that half a million of human beings were crowded into that labyrinth of lofty alleys, rich with shrines, and minarets, and balconies, and carved oriels, to which the sacred apes clung by hundreds. The traveler could scarcely make his way through the press of holy mendicants, and not less holy bulls. The broad and stately flights of steps which descended from these swarming haunts, and the bathing places along the Ganges, were worn every day by the footsteps of an innumerable multitude of worshipers. The schools and temples drew crowds of pious Hindoos from every province where the Brahminical faith was known. Hundreds of devotees came thither every month to die; for it was believed that a peculiarly happy fate awaited the man who should pass from the sacred city into the sacred river. Nor was superstition the only motive which allured strangers to that great metropolis. Commerce had as many pilgrims as religion. All along the shores of the venerable stream lay great fleets of vessels laden with rich merchandise. From the looms of Benares went forth the most delicate silks that adorned the balls of St. James and of Versailles; and in the bazaars, the muslins of Bengal and the sabers of Oude were mingled with the jewels of Golconda and the shawls of Cashmere."

Before daylight next morning we were in a carriage, and on our way to Sigra, the site of the Church mission. Thence we proceeded to the celebrated temples of Trilochan, Nirbadeshwar, Bisheshwar, Admahadeo, Gyanapi, etc. Going down to the river, we took a boat and rowed along the water-front of the city several miles, charmed with the palaces and ghats. Stopping at one of the latter, we saw a number of worshipers in the stream bathing and offering their devotions both to the water and the sun. Among these was an old woman with leprosy. On the bank sat a Fakeer, the most miserable object I ever beheld; wan, worn to a skeleton, his limbs apparently stiffened, his hair disheveled, his whole person nearly nude, and covered with ashes. And yet he was an object of worship as he stood silent and stupid before us. Passing by numerous temples we proceed to the center of the city to visit the Mosque of Aurungzebe, built on the site of the magnificent Hindoo temple, Bindoo Madhava, which was destroyed to give it place. Ascending one of its minarets, 232 feet, we had a pretty good view of the ecclesiastical capital of Hindostan, so holy in the estimation of Hindoos that any one dying within a circle of fifty miles of which a certain well in the city is the center, is sure of heaven. This brings multitudes from all quarters thither to die. It is the seat of the Hindoo Sanscrit College, the chief institution of native Hindoo learning, and it is crowded, not merely with scholars, but mendicant priests. We next visited the Man Mandil, an ancient Hindoo observatory, many of whose coarse but curious instruments are still preserved. Thence we passed through some of the narrow streets, a part of the Chowkambia bazaar, and the market Beseshergunje, the Queen's College, the College of Jay Narayen, and the schools of the missionaries.

One of the strangest objects to a Western man is the treatment of the dead. The corpse is taken in a palanquin to the bank of the stream; here it is sprinkled with Ganges water. A fire is kindled under it, the friends attending depart, and the persons having charge of the cremation do not wait for it to be consumed, but push it half charred into the river, down which it floats, the crows pecking it above, the fishes below.

Passing from temple to temple, and from shrine to shrine, we could but think what an awful thing Indian idolatry is. So filthy, so vile, Christian pen dare not describe what the eye may see in that classic seat of heathenism. You must read the first chapter of the Epistle to the Romans to understand it. The apostle meant what he said when he told the Ephesians that they were washed. Heathens now need washing, not their feet and hands alone, but their tongues, their minds, their consciences. It is *silly* as it is vile. Monkeys are venerated. In the neighborhood of one temple they crowd the street, the sidewalks, and hang from the roofs of the houses like grapes from the vine. They fill the courts and gates of the temple itself. Sacred bulls, too, wander the streets, fat and impudent and dangerous, helping themselves at the groceries, and turning the people from the sidewalks. Occasionally one is enticed aside by the Mohammedans, and slyly converted into beef. At one time the Government was obliged to deport a number across the river for the safety of the city. When a rich man loses a relative he lets loose a bull, which is supposed to be the recipient of the departed spirit, and thenceforward he becomes sacred. A bull, however, would be sacred without this, as this animal is supposed to be one of the forms of incarnation assumed by Vishnu; and the Ganges is supposed to proceed from the mouth of a cow. Images, as well as natural objects, are worshiped. Mr. Leupolt, a Church missionary, said that after riding all one day, in the most romantic and beautiful region of the valley of the Nerbuddah, charmed both with the waters and the fields, and especially the mountains, whose gorges seemed to lift the mind irresistibly up to the Almighty, he came across a Fakeer, who was in a dark, dirty cave, where he had dwelt alone for thirty years, worshiping an idol, which he had made himself. He was curious to see the object of the man's devotion; and what think you it was made of—cow-dung! Now, said Mr. L., if the man had spent life worshiping the mountains or the stream, I would have forgiven him, but to make his adoration day after day, year after year, to that bit of dirt, was too horrible.

The worship is a piece of mosaic. At one temple there stood at the gate a shivering ram, which some one had brought to be sacrificed to appease the god who was supposed to have brought sickness upon his family. Near by was the altar, and by its side the broad and bloody knife wherewith the priest is accustomed to sever, at a blow, the head of the animal from the neck. Passing into the court we see the temple. It is small. On a platform before it stands the priest; in the rear is the idol. The worshiper enters with some water and flowers. In order that the god may notice him and give attention to his offering, he rings the bell which is suspended above him. Having poured water and sprinkled flowers upon the object of his devotion, he sits down with a string of beads in his hands to count his prayers, which generally consist of a repetition of the word Ram—the name of his god. So shameful is the appearance of one of the common objects of worship that even Indian women, though veiled, are too modest to present themselves before it by daylight, and therefore they pay their devotions at night. Such is the tendency to worship that men are found worshiping telegraph poles, gas-pipes, and ordinary men who do any extraordinary deeds. It is easy to conceive what must be the literature and the common language of such a people. The curses and conversation of even the children in the street would not be repeated in the vilest purlieus of New York. If you ask the reason why the women are not educated, you are told that there is no literature in Hindoo fit for a decent woman to read. Of course the mind of the people is dwarfed and the conscience corrupted. As practice flows from principles, it must needs be that Indian morality is law. Notwithstanding the influence of British magistracy and the power of British laws, infanticide, slavery, dakoitee, thuggee, and other forms of wickedness are practiced, though concealed.

And yet there is hope for the people! Sir John Lawrence happened to be at Benares during my stay there, and four hundred pupils of the Queen's College, and four thousand children from the schools presented themselves before him on the grass of the campus with their slates and maps, and copy-books and diagrams, prepared to answer questions. One boy had advanced to the fourth book of Euclid. This visit of Sir John gave me an opportunity of seeing more of the higher life of India in one day than I could have done under ordinary circumstances in years. A party of one hundred and fifty persons, from the best families of the neighboring districts, came to the ball of the Maharajah of the city. The line of road through which his Excellency passed—six miles—was lighted with candles, the Ghat opposite to Ramnuggur was covered with white cloth, boats with fire-works were anchored in the stream, the fort was brilliantly illuminated, and the whole stream seemed ablaze. We were behindhand as to the ball, but not as to the *Durbar* which the Viceroy held on the following day for the purpose of investing the Rajah of Rewah with the star of India; an honor held in the highest estimation, and which was conferred on this occasion for fidelity to the British Government during the late Indian Rebellion.

The large tent of the Maharajah of Benares was pitched on the lawn for the purpose. The Indian dignitaries came in Oriental style. They themselves usually rode in elegant open carriages, guarded by cavalry and followed by long trains of attendants on camels or elephants. The scene outside the tent was bewildering. On all sides, drawn up in a hollow square, with perfect regularity and richly caparisoned, were cavalry, camels, and elephants, the arms and dresses of whose riders flashed in the sunbeams. Within were the carriages of the Rajahs and Nawabs, and between the two lines British infantry and artillery, under the marshaling of General Troup. Entering the tent early we had an opportunity of scanning the parties as they entered. The Viceroy's arm-chair, of solid silver, occupied the center of the tent, under an embroidered canopy, supported by four silver poles; on the right of this was another silver chair, set for the Rajah of Rewah, and on the left a third, for his Honor the Governor of the North-Western Provinces. To the right of the Lieutenant-Governor were chairs in five rows for the European ladies and gentlemen, one of which I occupied; and on the left side after the silver chair of his Highness, the Rajah of Rewah, were placed chairs for the other Maharajahs, Rajahs, Nawabs, Princes, and the nobility and gentry, each being seated according to his rank; all were dressed in the showy costume of the East, loaded with diamonds, "barbaric pearls, and gold;" some probably had a million's worth of property upon their persons. Among those near the top were pointed out to us two youthful Princes of the house of Delhi, the Princes of Nepaul, the Maharajah of Nizninagram, the Maharajah of Benares, and the Rajah Dwa Narajen, and Sing Bahadoor. The Star of India was placed on a velvet cushion on a table in the middle. The troops in the station formed a guard of honor. At half-past four, P. M., the Maharajah entered the tent under a salute of seventeen guns. Shortly after his Excellency entered under a royal salute, with blast of bugle and roll of drum; the band then played the national anthem.

His Excellency, after being seated a few moments, bid the Rajah rise, and addressed him in a short speech in Hindee, of which this is the substance:

"Forty years ago the British Government made a treaty with your ancestors. You have observed its conditions. In 1857 you behaved well; you belong to the tribe of Rajpoots, celebrated for their bravery. Lord Canning gave you jagheres; Her Majesty now confers upon you the most exalted Star of India, which will raise you in the eyes of all the Rajahs and Chiefs of Hindustan."

The Rajah, in his reply, acknowledged his obligations, depreciated his services, and pledged his life to the British Government. His Excellency then put the Star of India on the breast of the honored Chief, and the ceremony was over. After a moment's pause Sir John retired under a royal salute; the Rajah soon followed him, under the salute of his rank, and the rest of the assembly dispersed in due order. I paused a short time outside the tent, to see the carriages and cavalcades move off. Soon the long trains disappeared in the distance, covered with a cloud of dust which enveloped the whole horizon. I had seen much of high life in India, and was impressed not merely with the fine persons and brilliant equipages of the nobles, but with their elegant manners. I have never seen a man of more benign aspect and more courteous behavior than the Maharajah of Benares. To the favored Chief the day was the proudest one of his life; and yet, poor man, how miserable! His hands are bound up; he could not handle the Star he had received; he was a leper; he would give millions, and honors, and offices, and Star besides, to have the disease that was consuming him, and making him an object of horror to wife and children, arrested.

It is the policy of the British Government when they unseat native chiefs to attach them by stipends, and pensions, and honors. In the Bengal Presidency alone the Government treasury pays annually for this purpose 3,673,946 rupees, of which 1,249,901 goes to the family of Oude.

The festivals of the Hindoos are numerous, and embrace two things, worship and sport. The festival of the Dewalee occurred during my stay at Benares. It is the festival of lamps, and is celebrated in honor of Lukshmee, wife of

Vishnu, and the goddess of wealth. A day or two before the festival the people whitewash their houses, and when the day arrives they bathe themselves and put on clean clothes. In the evenings they illuminate their premises. The city on this occasion was in a blaze, the stores, streets, courts, and yards were filled with little lamps. One Christian, I am sorry to say, lighted up his compound. On this day merchants examine their accounts to see what have been the profits and losses of the year, and worship Lukshmee with their account books before them. In the evening thieves go out on trial trips. If they can steal any thing they take it as a good omen for the year; if they fail, as a bad one. Confectioners make various sweetmeats and preparations of fried rice to sell to the children, and cowherds paint the horns of their oxen red. The chief amusement of the festival is gambling, which is done openly.

Almost all labor is done with human muscles. In leaving Benares we employ coolies to bear our baggage to the station. Dr. Butler settled, but the bearers were not satisfied. An old woman of the company pursued him.

"Why," said he, "I have given you the wages of a day for a few minutes' work."

"Ah, but you have a Lord Padre in company."

Such was their idea of a Bishop. The coolies elsewhere claimed that I was equal to a general, and must give as much as he. But now we are on our way to Allahabad, the capital of the North-West; we go by railway to the Jumna. Here we find the bridge incomplete by reason of the difficulty of building one of the abutments. We are conveyed over the stream in a steamer, which takes soundings every few minutes, because of the perpetual shifting of the sands. Here we see multitudes of persons—men, women, and children—carrying sand and mud upon their heads, in little baskets, to lay a new foundation for the last abutment of the bridge. On our passage we were introduced to a celebrated Mohammedan, Syud Ahmud, Principal Sudder Ahmeen, or native judge of Allyghur, who, in the last rebellion, held the district of Bijnour against the Nawab of Nujubabad until obliged to take refuge in the cantonments of Meerut. In consideration of his services he receives a pension that descends to his eldest son. He is writing an elaborate commentary on the Old Testament Scriptures, which he holds to be inspired and binding on all Mohammedans. He combats the arguments of Colenso with great ability. He differs from Christians only in this, that he does not believe Christ, though a prophet, to be divine, and does believe Mohammed to be a prophet. We were met at the Ghat by the Chuprassee of Hon. Mr. Muir, one of the Governor-General's council, who placed us in a carriage and drove us to his master's, where we were entertained with princely hospitality, and met with many friends, among them Mr. Owen, of the American Board. On the next day we attended a meeting of the Directors of the Bible Society, the Tract Society, and the Anglo-Vernacular Education Society. Mr. Mohun, a native preacher, insisting on the Hindee language instead of the Ordu, which the British are trying to make the common medium, said: "You have taken away our country; will you take away our language also?"

We visited the Christian native school and village, and the printing-office of the American Mission, where we found native printers publishing, on their own account, "Bunyan's Pilgrim's Progress" and "Holy War."

III.

FROM ALLAHABAD TO AGRA.

LEAVING Allahabad we started for Cawnpore, 120 miles higher up on the railway. On arriving at the latter city we hired a carriage, and took a look at it. It contains over 100,000 people, is the seat of a large trade and extensive manufactures, and the terminus of the Ganges Canal. It is noted for an outrage committed in the rebellion of 1857. Gen. Wheeler took refuge in an intrenchment with 900 Europeans, most of whom were women and children. He was besieged by the Rajah of Bithoor, the Nana Sahib. When the Europeans were reduced to one-half their original number, and out of ammunition, they surrendered, under a promise of safe conduct to Allahabad, but the men were treacherously murdered, and the women and children confined. When the Nana heard of the approach of Havelock, he caused his prisoners to be massacred and thrown into a well. The Sepoys refused to do the savage work, and the Nana sent for the butchers of the city to execute his command. Over the well a massive and beautiful monument, with a richly carved screen of stone, has been erected, and around this a park has been laid out, with gravel walks, flower beds, and running waters.

I had the pleasure of traveling in company with Major Thompson, the only survivor of the Cawnpore massacre. He escaped by swimming for miles down the Ganges, fired upon from the shore.

From Cawnpore we proceed to Agra. This is a city of 100,000 inhabitants, and, until lately, the capital of the North-West Provinces. It was the seat of Mohammedan power in India in the days of the great Akbar. It is one of the keys of Northern Hindostan, and was a central position in the rebellion of 1857. It contains a fort a mile and a half in circuit, with battlements 70 feet high, within which is the palace of Akbar, and the Pearl Mosque. Two centuries ago this city was probably ten times the size that it is at present. Cultivated fields now occupy what once was covered with palaces, and the plowshare runs over the remains of baths, subterranean rooms, and other ruins of former palaces. We were received very kindly by Major Ward, Cantonment magistrate, who, with his family, had just returned from the hills, whither they had found it necessary to resort in order to recuperate.

The most remarkable object at Agra is the Taj Mahal. It is perhaps the most beautiful building on the earth. It stands on the left bank of the Jumna, two miles from the city It rises 296 feet from the platform to the crescent, and is visible a distance of twenty miles. Viewing it from the lofty tomb of Akbar, five miles distant, it looks like a tent of snowy whiteness and rich embroidery let down from heaven into a paradise of earth to be the audience-chamber of an angel on an errand of mercy to men. As you approach it you catch different views of it, but all charming. And now you are at the gate, which arrests your attention at once by the magnitude of its walls, the harmony of its proportions, and the chasteness and appropriateness of its ornaments. Around the lofty archway are Arabic letters in black marble, let into the red granite, constituting chosen texts of the Koran. Passing through the arch you find yourself in the hall, which reminds you of many passages of Oriental writings; such as, "The gates of hell shall not prevail against it;" for, within this gate, if angels were sent to recover Eden, Michael might hold a council of war, and from it send forth a troop to sweep the demons from the plains of the Ganges, which they have so long polluted. Ascending successive flights of stone steps, we gain the summit of the inner wall of the gate, and move forward to the center of a colonnade supporting a row of domes. Here we sit down, fronting the Taj, while every sense is intoxicated with enjoyment. Below and before us is a broad stream of water, extending from the gate to the platform of the building, like a section of a sea of glass laid as a pavement for the feet of the blest, and from whose tranquil surface the beauties of the Taj are doubled by reflection. On each side of this stream is a gravel walk, shaded by a row of cypress trees, whose perennial verdure is in striking contrast with the crystal surface on which they cast their shadows. Between these trees the choicest shrubs bloom, and at their feet humbler plants, children of the shade, display their modest beauty. Beyond them, on both sides, out to the lofty wall of the inclosure, the seisam, the neim, the plantain, the orange, the lemon, and the palm throw their shade, diffuse their fragrance, and drop their fruits; while here and there, where the sun finds a free passage among them for his beams, enchanting walks, bordered with richest flowers, invite the wandering feet. Birds of choicest plumage hop from branch to branch, while their companions of less attractive colors, but sweeter endowments, fill the air with delicious song. But what, above all, draws the attention is the building, whose polished marble walls, standing against the blue of heaven and the green of earth, give such strange charms to both, and receive from the contrast even more than they bestow. Descending to the hall of the gate, we pass through the inner arch, and proceed slowly up one of the graveled walks, to mingle with the pleasures of sense the higher pleasures of imagination and taste. Now we are upon the lofty platform. What breadth of beauty! To be impressed with the magnitude of the edifice we must walk the platform from end to end, and survey those massive buildings of red granite, which rise like sentinels, one on each side, corresponding exteriorly, but varied interiorly, to adapt them to their respective uses, the one being the hall of audience, the other the hall of prayer. Then mark the marble minarets, 225 feet high, one at each corner, rising as if to touch the clouds, and help us heavenward by their spiral staircases. Now we go from minaret to minaret all around the platform, and look up at the Taj, as we pass, at every side. No matter whether we view it at this angle or at that, in front or rear, on the right or the left, in one light, or a brighter, or a dimmer, we see fullness of beauty. What perfection of workmanship! Look all around the platform up the walls to the dome. There is no crevice, between the closely fitted stones, through which a spear of grass could find an entrance for its slender head. The meanest part of the pavement seems to have felt the touches of an artist worthy to build a throne, and the whole work, though it has been exposed to the sun and air and lightning for centuries, has not one stain upon its polished breast, but looks like a gem fresh from the hands of the lapidary.

What *combination* of charms! as if the architect had found out the secret of God how to blend massiveness with delicacy, unity with variety, simplicity with complexity, grandeur with beauty, and the utmost chasteness of design with surpassing skill of execution.

But let us enter the Taj. Now new charms break upon the sight. What strength and breadth in the arches! What symmetry throughout! What richness in the adornments! Mark the panels of the wall, how the marble is carved into the most exquisite forms of shrubs, and flowers in *alto-relievo.* Approach nearer and see that no two are alike, yet all are lovely.

Take any one for a minute inspection, that you may realize how grace waits upon every stem, and leaf, and blossom, and bud, and curve. Look from the panels up the wall to the bright star that beams upon you from the dome, and observe how by combinations of the agate, the amethyst, the blood-stone, and the carnelian inlaid in the marble, the artist has imitated the richest coloring as well as the most pleasing forms of nature, and you will be at a loss which most to admire, the exquisiteness of the drawings, the perfection of the execution, or the appropriateness of the designs. It is surprising that amid so much splendor there should be nothing gaudy; amid so much variety, nothing crowded; and amid such profusion of workmanship, nothing imperfect. Pass your finger over any part of any flower, or place your microscope upon it, and you will scarce detect where gem meets gem to blend their colors, and show that art may mold the stones of the mountains into combinations charming as those which Nature weaves to adorn the garment on her breast.

But look at that octagonal palisade in the center. Each side is a block of marble fretted by Florentine art, and bordered with mosaic, the whole constituting a screen which for its size, and for the depth, durability, and variety, and richness of its carving, surpasses any thing of the kind.

Enter its gate and you pass from the pleasures of imagination to the higher ones, awakened by moral beauty. The Taj is a tomb. It is the testimony of a rational soul to its own immortality. It is the sorrowing past pointing onward to the happy future. It is the memorial of love, a love inspired by beauty and a talent, unlike Cleopatra's, inspired by goodness. It is associated with purity too, for it is the memorial of wedded love.

Here is the tomb of the Queen Moomtaj-i-mahul, Ranoo Begum, for whom the building was erected, and by its side that of her royal husband, Shah Jehan—king of the world—who erected it. Both simple, white, not obtrusive, but concealed, like violets in a grove, to be sought for in order to be seen. Nothing strikes us more than the absence of all imagery here. Not a statue, nor a statuette, nor a painting of beast or idol, or man or angel—not a name, not even on the tombs, except the thousand names of God in black marble inlaid in the white on the monument of the Queen; as if the artist had woven and adorned a tent for God, but determined that nothing should share the space with him, or divert attention from his presence. As we stand

and muse, the heart swells, and the thought wells up, Lo, God is here! and we feel as if it would be a relief to weep.

We go out and sit down on the front steps, while the sun fringes the West with those orange robes so peculiar to the lands of the East. The fragrant air is stirred only by the evening flutter of the birds which serve to mark the stillness, and silence, and peace that reign around. The subdued light seems to add new charms to the gorgeous coloring of the Oriental flowers, while the water that wells up from the Jumna and through its polished basin rolls in a calm, broad crystal stream from the platform to the gate, through the midst of the garden, reminds us of the river of life. Soon the moon comes forth attended by her train, showing the beauties of the Taj, softened in her beams. Now let us enter the building again. The magistrate, who kindly attends us, has, without our knowledge, sent thirteen or fourteen coolies before us, to stand in the arches above and below. At a signal each kindles a Bengal light, in whose mingled blaze the brilliant stones and polished marble are reflected. Presently, as the lights burn dim, and while we stand within the palisade, beside the official tombs, looking up at the star of the dome directly overhead, a native, who had gone down into the dark vault in which the ashes of the noble dead are inurned, utters a few solemn words that come up like an organ peal, and go echoing from arch to arch, majestic as distant thunder, but varied as the aerial harp, like the spirit of the past coming up from the grave, and lingering around the memorials of its love before it reascends to God.

We seem to be in the presence of the charming Momtaza Tumanee—she of the divinely delicate face, with an eye more beautiful than the evening star, and locks clustering on her bosom more decorative than the feathers of the peacock. We call to mind that terrible day when the palace was oppressed, and the servants were afraid, and the physicians were assembled, and the ministers' wives gathered silently in the chamber, and the priests with tremulous voices read prayers, and the trembling nurses rubbed the feet and hands of the poor Empress, and the Emperor racked his mind for words of solace and comfort to the Queen, and when, at last, she ordered her gems and jewels to be brought to her bedside, and said: "Pardon all my faults, and every unkind word. I have lived with you through joy and sorrow. God has made you a great Emperor, and given you worlds to rule, and sons and daughters to perpetuate your name; but now I must leave you, and be a traveler to worlds unknown. Build me such a tomb as the world never saw." And the parting husband and wife wept and convulsively laughed and cried as they talked of death, and the promise was made and received.

Round all things human cluster painful associations. Passing out of the building a native says: "Alas! how many admire this structure who consider not the tears and toils in which it was built!" During seventeen years 20,000 workmen were forced to labor upon it without compensation, and even their rations were curtailed by rapacious officials, so that great distress and unusual mortality prevailed among them. Could this beautiful marble tell its own story, it might be one of sighs and tears. The noblest productions in art, in science, and in song are generally pressed from crushed souls. Besides this enforced labor, $8,750,000 was taken from the capital of the country when money was from three to five times its present value.

There is another painful consideration connected with the Taj. Though complete in itself, it is only a part of the design of the Emperor. He intended to erect a tomb for himself on the opposite side of the river of equal beauty and magnificence with his wife's, and to connect the two by a bridge with railings of solid silver; but the children, on whose account, in accordance with their mother's dying request, he abstained from a second marriage, proved ingrates, inaugurated civil wars, imprisoned their aged father, put out his eyes, and crippled his empire. Rarely is it given in this world to perfect a grand design.

IV.

AGRA TO DELHI.

FROM Agra we went by Ghary to Futteporė Sikra. On the way we were hindered by a balky horse; which reminds us that all the horses in India are poor, except such as are imported from Cabul or from England, and these can not perform much service on account of the heat of the country. They are seldom driven more than ten miles at a time. A syce attends each horse, running behind the carriage. A syce can go much farther in a day than any horse. When the horse has completed his journey the syce feeds him, covers him, and walks him home. If you keep two horses in India you must have two syces; but it must be remembered that the syce cuts the grass for the horse the year round. Hay is not provided, as it is not necessary. The horses to be hired at the livery stable or dak are very poorly managed. We seldom hired a horse ghary without having trouble and delay. The driver often used the poor brute shamefully, and in return it displayed its obstinacy.

The distance from Agra to Futtepore Sikra is twenty-two miles. The road is bordered for some distance with stately trees. This place was the Buckingham Palace of Akbar, deservedly surnamed the Great; for he was the noblest of all the emperors of Hindostan. He diminished taxes, tolerated all religions, promoted agriculture, extended commerce, improved the roads, reformed the government, and extended the boundaries of his empire.

We approach the palace through a mass of ruins, which indicate the magnificence that reigned here at a former period. The buildings are on a grand scale, and the views on all sides are enchanting. In passing around the palace three or four objects were particularly noticeable: the stables and out-houses indicated a large stud of horses and flock of elephants; the platform where the monarch sat to watch the boys diving for the coin he threw into the water; the building in which the ladies of the Zenana played hide-and-seek; the hall in which the emperor received embassadors; the diwan e'khaz, in which he held his cabinet counsels; the diwan e'am, in which, each morning, he made his public appearance, and the court where he sat before his Bachise board, consisting of blocks of black and white marble, to play backgammon with his prime minister, using his wives for ivory blocks, and making them trot from square to square as the moves were made, are all well preserved. We noticed, also, a separate building in the Zenana, covered with paintings in fresco by Persian artists, for a Christian wife. She was a Portuguese, and is said to have had great power over him. Among the decorations of religious meaning in her apartments some are Christian. At the foot of the hill is the small village of Futtepore, which was probably built of materials gathered from the ruins. The palace was completed in 1751. The architecture is massive, Saracenic, and every part of it is elaborately carved. The grandest part is the Dur gah or tomb of the Sheikh Selim Chiste. This, and the canopy over it, is of mother of pearl, the floor is of jasper, and the walls are of marble inlaid with carnelian. It is inclosed by screens of marble of great richness. It stands in a paved court 428 feet by 406 feet, which is entered by a gateway 120 feet high. In its center is a fountain and tank, and on one side a mosque with triple dome. The tomb was covered with fresh flowers, and decorated with shreds of cloth, so that you might imagine it to be, as it probably was to thousands, an object of worship.

The palace is occupied by an agent of the Government, who furnishes entertainment for visitors at reasonable rates. After tiffin, while we were seated for repose, a native brought to us a tiger which he had just caught. It was young, and we took it in our hands, but, as it showed its teeth, we were very glad to get rid of it. The happy captor doubtless soon slew his prize, and received from Government a reward for his scalp. The incident reminded us of the story that Selim, the holy man, first obtained his reputation by his intimacy with tigers, several of which lived with him in a cave on the spot now occupied by his tomb. We returned in good time to Agra. Next day we went to Secundra, the seat of a large orphanage under the patronage of the Church of England. We attended the Church service in the morning, and breakfasted afterward with Mr. Barbul, the missionary.

The printing-press of this mission occupies the tomb of the Christian wife of Akbar, Begum Munni. We next proceeded to Akbar's tomb, near by. This is in a square garden inclosed with a wall pierced by four gateways of red sandstone seventy feet high, one on each side, whence four stone walks lead to an elevated platform from which the tomb rises. This platform is of solid stone, and four hundred feet square. The tomb is square also, three hundred feet on each side, and rises in five terraces to the height of one hundred feet. The upper story is of white marble, the rest of red sandstone. From the main entrance we proceed to a vaulted hall in the center, where the sarcophagus of Akbar is seen.

On the top of the edifice there is a platform open to the sky surrounded by a marble screen richly carved, and on this platform, beneath a marble pavilion, is the second or official tomb. This is beautifully carved. There are turrets at each corner of this terrace. From this elevated spot we had a view of Agra and of the Taj.

Returning to Agra we dined with Rev. Mr. Grierson, of the Baptist mission, and in the evening preached in his chapel to a good audience of citizens and soldiers. Next day we started for Delhi, having a good railway all the distance. We had been invited in advance to enjoy the hospitalities of Mr. Parry, manager of the Delhi Bank, and his chuprassie met us at the station. His residence is in an extensive garden, and was formerly the palace of Begum Sombre. Our first look at Delhi was through the Chandnee Chowk, a broad and beautiful avenue, a mile long and 120 feet wide, comparable, almost, to the Parisian boulevards, and intersected by a canal or aqueduct in the center. It is ornamented with trees, and, at times, crowded with visitors. Many of the buildings are historical; among them, we were pointed to the mosque of Rooshun-ood-Dowlah, where Nadir Shah sat during the massacre of the city, in which from 800,000 to 1,000,000 people were murdered, and where, too, he received Mahmoud Shah, the emperor, accompanied by his nobles, who, bursting into tears, besought him to spare the lives of his people. From this city the Persian conqueror is said to have carried away fifty millions of dollars in money, besides gold and silver plate worth millions more, jewels of inestimable value, and the peacock throne, valued at six million pounds sterling. Along this street you see stores of every description, and artisans at work manufacturing those articles for which the city is so famous. Its works in gold and silver are unsurpassed, and its shawls and scarfs are surpassed only by those of Umritsir and Lahore.

The modern city is on the western bank of the Jumna, and was founded by Shah Jehan in 1620. It is surrounded by brick walls, and is about seven miles in circumference. There is another fine street, five furlongs in length, and ninety feet in breadth, leading from the Palace to the Delhi gate.

In the evening we took a drive to see some noticeable objects. We first went to the arsenal so memorable for its connection with the mutiny of 1857. The mutineers from the first fixed their minds upon Delhi, because it was the richest city in the North-West Provinces, well walled and fortified, and possessed of the grandest arsenal and the richest treasury in Upper India. The British were taken by surprise when the troops mutinied and shot down their officers, and all other Europeans within their reach. A few English officers were in the magazine when it was assailed. The spot was pointed out where Forrest and Buckley together loaded and fired in rapid succession four rounds from three six-pounders and a howitzer, which had been hastily got into position to command the gate of the magazine. They were fired on by hundreds at a distance of fifty yards. As the last round was fired, musket balls disabled both of the gunners. Lieutenant Willoughby then gave orders to fire the magazine, and they were obeyed. We next proceed to the point where General Barnard, on his approach to the siege, found the rebels posted, and whence he drove them within the walls; next to the crest, a mile and a half from the city, taken up by the British forces when they commenced the siege; then to the point on which they planted three batteries, half a mile nearer, to play day and night upon the city wall, the mutineers all the while replying with three batteries; then we proceeded to the breach in the wall, near the Cashmere gate, through which the troops rushed after it was blown open. The troops once entered, marched along the ramparts to the Moree bastion and Cabul gate, where the carnage was the most fearful, and the victory decisive.

After this we took a drive into the gardens of the late King of Delhi.

Next day, taking an early start, we drove out to see the Khuttub Minar, the grandest column of the world. It is eleven miles from the city. The drive is a gloomy one, for it is amid ruins and tombs. Arches, walls, columns crumbling, piles of masonry are to be seen in every direction; grass and shrubbery make their way through the rubbish, and deserted buildings, and tombs; but the land, for an immense circuit, seems spoiled, since the plow could hardly make a passage through the bricks, sandstone, and mortar; and jackals and foxes have undisturbed possession. All this is easily accounted for. The city has been frequently moved to gratify the vanity of monarchs, and frequently destroyed to satisfy the ambition of conquerors and the love of spoil. We stop, after driving six miles, to see the tomb of Suftar Jung, the founder of the royal house of Oude. It is very fine, and similar to the Taj, though by no means equal to it. From the top of it the Khuttub Minar is visible, though we must drive five miles further to reach it. It is a round pillar 240 feet high, thirty-five feet at the base, but diminishing gradually to about ten feet at the top. It has five stories, decreasing in height in the same proportion as the diameter of the shaft. The three lowest stories are of red sandstone, fluted and belted by bands of Arabic inscriptions; the two upper stories are of white marble. Each story has a stone balustrade, and a richly sculptured and heavy cornice. We ascend the shaft by a winding staircase of 378 steps. Returning to the base we reviewed it again at different distances. When it was built, by whom, and for what purpose, are questions to which we could get no answers, but the presumption is, I think, that it was begun, if not completed, by the Hindoos, and adopted and modified by the Mohammedans. A short distance to the North of it is the beginning of another shaft of larger dimensions. Near by are the ruins of a most gorgeous Hindoo temple, which seems subsequently to have been changed into a mosque. The arcades are supported by hundreds of columns all tastefully and elaborately carved.

Returning to Delhi we drove directly to the Jumna Musjid. It stands at the junction of four streets, and on an elevated platform. We pass unobstructed up the broad flight of steps, and walk the courts, and ascend one of the minarets to survey the famous city. This mosque is perhaps regarded by the Mohammedans with more pride and veneration than any building in India. It is worthy of admiration alike for its magnitude, its beauty, and its associations. We reached home weary and hungry. After dinner we go to the site of the palace. The outer wall is unimpaired, and the massive gates stand, but the palace is demolished. The scene, however, presents other things well worthy of attention—the pearl mosque, the throne-room, and the diwan. The mosque is a most exquisite piece of workmanship. It is of the purest white marble, with saracenic arches and three domes. It is beautiful from its form and portions, but without any gaudy or doubtful ornament, simple, pure, chaste, stainless—fitted to be a shrine for the Holy One.

The diwan is an arcade formed of three rows

of arches, with a marble pavilion in the center, inlaid with gold and precious stones. The roof is said to have been solid silver, but when the Mahrattas took Delhi they tore it off and bore it away as spoil. It is now of some other material. The columns are very massive and grand. Here the ancient Mogul emperors gave audience to embassadors, and received their obeisance. It is now occupied as a museum.

V.

A VIEW OF OUR INDIAN MISSIONS.

GENERAL REMARKS.

WE rarely feel much interest in what we do not see. Next to seeing is the report of an eye-witness. With a view to awaken in our brethren a deeper interest in the missions they sustain, I undertake a pen portrait of our mission stations in Hindostan.

In the year 1857 Rev. Dr. Butler was sent out to found an Indian mission for the Methodist Episcopal Church. He was the man for the work—prudent, pious, sagacious, with a courteous bearing, a just self-respect, an enterprising spirit, and a profound regard to the authorities by whom he was commissioned. By his selection of a field, choice of stations, management of the finances, and general oversight of the work, he evinced eminent abilities; and although, in consequence of a want of facility in inspiring in others the spirit of obedience and respect for official superiors, which was both a sentiment and habit with himself, and did not, perhaps, call forth the affection of his fellow-laborers to the extent to which he was entitled to it, yet he could but provoke their admiration at the proud monument which, in departing from India, he left behind him.

In October, 1864, he met me at Calcutta, and proceeded with me by railway up the Ganges, about eleven hundred and fifty miles, to Delhi.

FROM DELHI TO MEERUT.

Leaving the railway at this celebrated city at 11 o'clock, P. M., we started by horse *ghary* to Meerut. As the traveling in Hindostan, in consequence of the heat, is by night, the conveyances afford facilities for sleeping. On our way we encountered a cyclone of dust, so dense as to be almost suffocating. The driver, evidently alarmed, stopped, and inquired what should be done; but he was told to keep on as long as he could find the road. In about an hour we got out of the circle.

MEERUT TO BIJNOUR.

After taking a cup of tea at Meerut, we started by dhooley dak for Bijnour.

The dhooley is not, as Burke supposed, a wild

animal, but a cheap palanquin. It is carried by four men, who are relieved every half mile by four others, preceded by a *musalche,* bearing a lamp, for the double purpose of lighting the way and keeping off wild beasts, and followed by a *bangy wallah,* carrying the luggage on a bamboo, and are discharged after running about ten miles, satisfied with about eight cents wages each and bukshish, though sometimes they will run two *chowkies* for double pay. Experienced travelers can sleep in the dhooley, but not others. The noise of the bearers, as if distressed, the motion of the vehicle as they rushed forward, the shifting of the bamboo from shoulder to shoulder, the torch, every now and then flashing in the face, the conversation of the coolies, and their shouts when they feared a wild beast, or approached a relay, drove sleep from my eyes and slumber from my eyelids. When morning came we were threading our way, through water and mud, over stubble ground, newly plowed fields, along hedges and mud walls. The opening of the Ganges canal on the country, in consequence of the drought, so impaired our path that we did not reach Bijnour until ten o'clock next day.

When for the first time I saw the dhooley, I thought, what a mercy that I, instead of some of my colleagues, was sent! But when I saw my companion appropriating the shelves in my vehicle, on which he was stowing away bread, bacon, pots, and kettles, I found that I was to be brought up to a respectable weight avoirdupois, and that our two sets of coolies had their burdens equalized. While we cooked breakfast by the roadside, the coolies, seated some distance off in a circle, smoked the hooka, the stem of which they passed from mouth to mouth.

BIJNOUR AND ITS OUT-STATIONS.

Arriving at Bijnour, a provincial city of Rohilcund, we were kindly met by Rev. I. L. Hauser, the missionary. Our first attention is given to the school. The average attendance is eighty-nine, all boys. There are five teachers; namely, two Hindoos, two Mohammedans, and one Christian. The head master is a Hindoo, but the school is opened with prayer and the reading of the Bible. Pagan and Mussulman teachers will teach the Holy Scriptures as ours do Homer. An examination of the classes in the ordinary branches and the Bible was quite satisfactory. The mission-house, of brick covered with cement, sixty-four feet by seventy-four, with verandas, stands upon a tract of eighteen acres. It cost $3,250, and is valued at $2,650. Near by is a bungalow belonging to the mission, situated on a tract of two acres. Cost, $425; present value, $300. A school-house, sixty-four feet front by seventy-four deep in the clear, with veranda before and behind, each ten feet wide, is building. Its main walls are two feet thick, and it stands on an inclosure of two acres. There are two native helpers' houses, which cost $150, now worth $75. The chapel, used as a school-house, is worth $100. There is also chapel furniture, $42; school requisites, $160; tents, etc., $78; other property, $10. The whole land belonging to this mission is twenty-two acres. The deeds are quit-claim, and subject to an annual rent. The Government gives $1,875 toward the erection of a school-house, and requires the rest to be paid by subscription. This building is suitable and substantial, and if finished according to the original plan will be ornamental. In taking subscriptions for it, the preacher promised that it should be used for scholastic purposes only, his object being twofold; namely, to increase the liberality of the non-Christian citizens, and put the Christian under bonds to build a church.

The number of members at this station is ten, excluding the missionary and his wife, all adults; there are seven probationers, also adults. Class-meetings and prayer-meetings and Sabbath-school are held weekly; the last numbers but twenty-four pupils. Love-feast once a quarter. On Sabbath we have English preaching at half-past 7, A. M.; native Sabbath-school, half-past 9, A. M.; Hindoo preaching, 5, P. M. Wednesday evening, English Bible-class. Mrs. H. teaches a school of native girls at her own house. There were six baptisms during the year. There is an English congregation of about twenty-six persons. I took occasion during my stay here to visit the house of a native gentleman who belongs to the merchant caste, and has grown rich by lending money at from 23 to 30 per cent. per annum. In it I found a room consecrated to his idol, and on that part of the roof which covered it I was cautioned not to step, as it is holy ground. The gardens were showy, and abounded in marigolds. On the way back we passed a beautiful tomb, inclosed with brick, planted with flowers, and built for a courtesan by her Mohammedan admirers, who, if their wives were to die, would probably show but little respect to their graves. Our next visit was to the jail, to which the magistrate kindly attended us. An armed guard followed us from department to department, and whenever we stopped drew up behind us, to prevent an attack, a precaution as necessary as if we were moving among tigers. The prisoners are engaged in various manufactures. For minor offenses whipping is the penalty, as confinement, if caste be preserved, is not dreaded; some, indeed, are pleased with it, and one, on being discharged, asked in distress for what offense he was turned away. Cattle stealing is practiced extensively by companies at great distances, who exchange spoil with each other.

Before leaving I delivered a discourse—Mr. H. interpreting—and administered baptism to four persons, and the sacrament of the Lord's-Supper to thirteen natives and some others. While seated in the parlor one day I could but congratulate Mrs. H. on her spacious and beautiful home, its nice furniture, beautiful gardens, and ample stores; but, alas! every one knoweth his own sorrows! She had but lately laid in the grave her youngest child, and the remaining one, as well as herself, was but slowly recovering from diphtheria; and when she said, "What should I do if my husband should die?" I saw the tear starting; and as I replied, "Trust God and his Church," I thought it good to take the fresh air.

NUJEEHABAD.

Setting off at nine o'clock at night we move onward for Nujeebabad, an out-station of Bijnour. Severe shaking, perpetual chattering, no sleep. At 4 o'clock, A. M., we arrive at the city, encamping at daylight in front of the deserted palace of the Nawab, who, during the rebellion, forfeited his property and life. While Dr. B. cooks breakfast, Mr. Hauser and I explore. The palace is in ruins, but the Summer-house is in repair. Some things particularly attracted attention; among them, the platform where the Nawab surveyed the women bathing, watching for Bathshebas; the Zenana, which was dark, with lower apartments open toward the court, closed toward the exterior, without a window or an aperture in the wall, though with niches for the lamps; and the Government distillery, where any one may come and make arrack or sherab by paying twelve annas a gallon. It is made from the juice of the sugar-cane, which is fermented in cow-dung vats, then transferred to a rude still, and received, after distillation, in earthen pots sunk in the ground.

Before the English entered the country the natives were temperate; but now, despite their religion, they are indulging in both liquor and opium.

After breakfast we visited our school. It is in an open court, in which is no fire at any period of the year. It is taught by Mohammedans and Pagans, the head master being a Brahmin. I proposed prayer, but was told it was not admissible; called for a class in the Bible, but there was none prepared; asked a large class if any one could recite the ten commandments, but found none; examined classes in reading, grammar, arithmetic, and geography, and found that although in pronunciation and orthography the scholars were imperfect, they in other respects acquitted themselves well. Since my visit the missionary assures me that the school is on more Christian foundations. I noticed a number of citizens at the school, among them the magistrate or headman, and the doctor. The latter took us to his hospital, where he has several house patients, and prescribes for many out ones. He has received a medical degree, and performed most of the operations of surgery. He rarely uses the lancet, but his dispensary contains many active remedies, such as iodide of potassium, mercury, and quinine. Being a widower, he allowed us to enter his house, where we found his only child, a girl eight years old, seated upon the floor, decorated with gold ear-rings, and toe-rings, and silver bangles. She arose and recited the Lord's Prayer as the highest compliment she could bestow upon us; after which the doctor, bowing down and placing his face to the floor, asked what good he should do to me.

At eleven o'clock we are off for Nugeenah, where we have a school and a native helper's house, worth $150. Here, at the bungalow, I was taken sick, but stimulus, applied both internally and externally, so far revived me that I was enabled to pursue my journey the same day, but without examining the school at Nugeenah, which, however, is similar to that at Nujeebabad. The latter city is the larger, containing 20,000 inhabitants. From it may be seen the lower ranges of the Himalayas, twenty miles distant, as the crow would fly. Between the mountains and the town is jungle, in which tigers, boars, and elephants abound.

MORADABAD AND ITS OUT-STATIONS.

From Nugeenah we move on to Gurmaktezer, passing through Chandpoor—city of the moon—about midnight, and reaching at seven o'clock next morning the *Mela*, a great annual religious gathering or camp-meeting on the holy stream of the Ganges, where we were received by our missionary, Parker. Intoxicated with strange sights and sounds, we rode along the tents far down the river, on which were encamped six or seven hundred thousand people. Happily, among the sounds was the Gospel's joyful one, which we heard in the native tongues from the lips of missionaries at different parts of the encampment, and which was listened to with apparent interest by the groups of natives that gathered round the speakers. O what an opportunity to preach Jesus!

Now, off for Moradabad, forty miles distant, which we reached about ten o'clock the next day. On Sabbath we have love-feast. As I entered the congregation salaamed. The women and men sat apart, both neatly dressed. The speaking was prompt and brief; the singing in tunes, some native, some American, but all melodious and sweet. The whole service indicated that the people are rising to American civilization, and getting an idea of spiritual religion, one of the hardest things for them to comprehend, accustomed, as they have been, to a religion of mere ceremonies. I addressed them through an interpreter. Messrs. Parker, Mansell, Cawdell, and their wives, were present. At ten o'clock Mr. Cawdell preached. Several teachers and scholars from the City Mission School were present, some of them Hindoos and some Mohammedans. The communicants of this Church are all living on our ground, and in our employ. The native preachers and exhorters, however, live elsewhere. Our members are well instructed, being gathered together every evening for a Bible class.

There are small Christian congregations in the villages, but they are not well trained. How to get converts that are beyond the range of European employ is the great problem of the missions. At three o'clock we have Bible class and Sabbath-school. At the close each pupil recites a verse of Scripture. At four o'clock preaching in the bazaar in the center of the city to three or four thousand natives. Five or six hundred gathered close around to listen. They were respectful and attentive, and the boys in front behaved admirably. Two exhorters, one native preacher, and brothers Mansell, Cawdell, and Parker, delivered in succession, from a public well, short, animated discourses, like the successive peals of artillery. The city is better built than Indian cities usually are. It contains fifty-six thousand inhabitants, one-fourth of whom are said to be Mohammedans. The Hindoos, even the Brahmins, appear to tolerate and almost befriend us; but the Mussulmans are very bitter against us. Both classes have been moved to action by our bazaar preaching, and propound questions to us publicly, the Mussulmans often offensively. While the latter admit much revealed truth, they deny the divinity of Christ, and are obstinate fatalists. We quote against them the Koran, which declares him an infidel who denies the inspiration of the New Testament, or makes any distinction among the prophets. Mohammedans proclaim no atonement, and rely for salvation on the intercession of the prophet alone. Among the interesting incidents of our visit was the baptism of two children, and the administration of the Lord's-Supper to thirty-three native communicants and eight missionaries. A collection, as usual, was taken up. During the year, sixty-five dollars have been given by the members for the mission, besides the support of a native helper, notwithstanding the entire wages of each head of a family is but two dollars per month. The Christians here belong to the lowest caste of the Sikhs. When some of their head men joined the Christian Church, they, considering it equivalent to a change of caste, were ready to follow. Four or five hundred of this people own themselves Christians, and might become such under suitable instruction.

The property of the station consists of three and a half acres, for which a warranty deed in fee simple is held. On this plot are, 1. A substantial house, seventy feet square, containing fourteen rooms in all, valued at $2,000; 2. A chapel, ninety feet long, twenty feet wide, built of sun-dried brick, with a pulka roof. It is valued at $625. The servants' houses on the mission compound are included in the estimate for the house. The chapel furniture is valued at $49; itinerating requisites, $78; miscellaneous, $11; school-house, $18; school-house furniture in rented premises, $20.

In this city reside Mr. Huntingdon, British magistrate, and Mr. Power, district judge, by whom we were kindly received. The prayer-meetings of the mission are well attended, and appear to be devotional. At the close of one I was presented with a cane by some orphan boys, and with a purse by the first native female teacher employed in our school.

SUMBHAL.

On November 15th, at four o'clock in the morning, I started with Messrs. Parker and Mansell for Sumbhal, an out-station, distant twenty-two miles. The country is fruitful and beautiful. We arrived at our destination for breakfast at brother Cawdell's. Here our premises consist of an acre and a half of land, on which a mission house is building, at a cost of $300. The ground was purchased for us from Brahmins by the mayor or Tyceldar, who will receive the money, and put it into the hands of some person from whom they can secretly get it, as it is contrary to their rules to buy or sell. The city is very old and much scattered, but contains 15,579 inhabitants. Among its ancient buildings is a mosque, said to have been built three hundred and fifty years ago, on the site marked out as the place for the next and last incarnation of Vishnu. When the Mohammedans demolished the temple that once crowned the holy place, the Hindoos built another near by, in hope that the coming savior will accept it for the original. We have a school here, which was found creditable. It is under the superintendence of Ambica Churn, one of our native helpers, who has several ushers, none of whom, I am sorry to say, are Christians. Our next station is Babukhera, fourteen miles distant; our journey thither was by night. We missed our road, and had to seek the watchman of a village through which we passed to guide us. Arriving at our destination, we sank to rest in a tent which Mrs. Parker had set up for us. The place is a small one, containing one thousand inhabitants, dwelling in mud huts, and farming the neighboring land. The Christians here and in the vicinity are about eighty in number. We held service next morning, at eight o'clock, in the unroofed church which they are building, at a cost of $200, and where, after preaching, I baptized twenty-seven persons, who all seemed delighted with their initiation, of which they desired certificates.

After meeting I was presented with various little gifts from the children, and also a cane from a banyan-tree, held sacred by Mohammedans, as marking the tomb of a Mussulman martyr. This was the gift of our oldest convert, of whom Mr. Parker, under date May 9, 1866, gives the following account:

"You will doubtless remember, that while you were at Babukhera, when our little chapel was dedicated, a very old man from among our Christians there presented you with a cane. He was the oldest of all our Christians in this district, and probably the oldest Christian in our mission, and was like a father to all our people in his village. I write now to tell you of his death, the news of which has just reached us. He passed to his home on the 23d of April last, aged about eighty-six years. He was among the first of his tribe—the Sikhs—to embrace Christianity, and has ever since been among the most true and faithful Christians of India. He was uneducated, could not even read or write at all; yet he received Christianity—not as so many ignorant people in India do, as a change of caste, but as a *religion* of purity and holiness of heart and life. Our converts readily renounce idolatry, yet the *principles* and *practices* of idolatry often have to be rooted out gradually. But Father Dershni Singh, although he had practiced the deceptions of idolatry to his eightieth year, so received Christ that from his baptism to his death he lived a consistent Christian life. He always seemed ready to do what he could to help others in the true way. His influence was very great over the little class of his village, and, indeed, over all the Christians of his tribe; and, as he always tried to use this influence for good, he was a great help to us in our work.

"When we endeavored to establish a Christian colony in Wesleypoor, he went with his people there, and was a great help to us in commencing the work, and in keeping the people together. His wife died during the sickness there, and his eldest son, an excellent man, and an exhorter, also passed away there.

"In his Christian life he counted three important events. The first, his baptism; to receive which he walked nearly fifty miles in the eightieth year of his age, and was so thankful and happy that in his old age he had received the true Savior, and had been received by his people.

"The second was the visit of the bishop to his little village, and the dedication of the little chapel on his land, so long devoted to idolatry; and, to him, it added much to the interest of the event that the bishop, on the day of the dedication, baptized twenty-seven of his people, and that his grandson, who was baptized, was permitted to receive the name of the bishop.

"The third was our camp-meeting, held last November, where Father Dershni received a fuller baptism of the Holy Spirit than he had enjoyed before. His heart then became melted, and he rejoiced with joy unspeakable. Although so old, he remained with us during the entire meeting, and attended every service, early and late, to the end. Since that time, I have felt that he was growing up into Christ, and being perfected for his home. For some weeks past he has felt that he could not live long, and has talked freely of his death, and has always expressed himself as ready to depart.

"'How can I have fear,' said he to me the last time I was at his house, 'when all my trust is in Christ, the *true Savior?*' The native preacher at Babukheṙa writes that he continued in this same *confident*, trusting, happy spirit until the end.

"His life was a 'living *epistle*,' and his death confirmed the epistle of his life to all around him.

"As he had always been a man of influence

among his people, many gathered at his death, determined to have their usual ceremonies in spite of the Christians. He had, however, anticipated this, and had charged all his friends so strictly that they desisted, and his wish was carried out in a simple Christian burial."

NYNEE TAL AND THE MOUNTAINS.

We must now turn attention to another station; but, as Moradabad is not out of our way, we return to it, and tarry long enough to visit its mission schools, of which Mr. Mansell has charge. In clean, whitewashed apartments, we found about one hundred and fifty boys, dressed for the occasion, who, though somewhat deficient in Scripture, passed a satisfactory examination. Returning to the mission house, we had an opportunity of seeing the thronging population of the city, which our companion, an English engineer, and friend of our mission, did not hesitate to drive with his long whip, scarcely checking his strong Cabul steed in its passage through the mass that crowded the thoroughfares.

Left Moradabad in the dhooley by night, and arrived at Kaladoonge by six o'clock next day. We are now out of Rohilcund and in Kumaon. I was disturbed during the night by the shouting of the coolies in concert, which, we learned in the morning, was to keep off the tigers as we passed through the Terai. Getting out of the dhooley we found five or six elephants chained, whose drivers were just getting ready to start, having spent the night near our stopping place. We start up the hills and reach Mongolia, a travelers' rest-house, where Mrs. Butler, who had come down from Nynee Tal the previous evening to meet us, has prepared our breakfast. Having refreshed ourselves, we continued our journey up the mountain. When within two or three miles of Nynee Tal we saw Mr. and Mrs. Baume and two of their sons on a precipice, waving their handkerchiefs.

While here we dined with the Lieutenant-Governor of the North-West Provinces, who estimates their population at twenty-eight millions, and thinks the Mohammedans as one to five. Our mission property is eight and a half acres, four acres and a half of which is unoccupied, on which is a house, a chapel, and a school-house. The last is valued at $1,750; the mission house at $1,987; native helper's house, $225; chapel, $2,500; six school-houses, $2,375; a cemetery, $125; chapel requisites, $144; school requisites, $60; miscellaneous, $44. The chapel seems to me over-estimated, some of the other property under-estimated. Here is the place for a sanitarium, which, since my return, has been built. Our mission residence, though large, is old and out of repair. Our native congregation consists of forty-five members, who enjoy one service on the Sabbath, and usually attend the Sabbath-school, where they receive instruction as valuable as preaching. We have bazaar preaching from two to four times a week, when the season is favorable. One of our members, John Barker, is an exhorter. During the Summer we have several schools, some toward the foot of the hills. The average attendance is, at Nynee Tal, 45; Bheemtal, 35; Akotah, 30; Kaladoonge, 15; Huldwani, 40; Golapar, 12. All these are taught by heathen teachers, under the supervision of missionaries. The Scriptures are, however, read in them all, and the Nynee Tal school is opened with prayer. There is an English congregation in our church every Sabbath afternoon, with an average attendance of seventy-eight or eighty persons. Mrs. Baume teaches a female school, which has an average attendance of eighteen native children from the bazaar.

Not far from the town is the mission graveyard, consisting of an acre and a half of ground, the gift of the commissioner. It is in a sightly spot, grandly encompassed, though near to landslides and mountain gorges. It has been walled on three sides and fenced on the other, at a cost of $125. Here are the graves of Mrs. Thoburn, one of Dr. Butler's children, and one of Mr. Pierce's, suitably ornamented with shrubbery, which I found protected for the Winter by matting.

On Sabbath Mr. Baume preached to a native congregation of eleven, mostly servants and children. After preaching came Sabbath-school. At four o'clock I preached to a good English congregation, including the Lieutenant-Governor and his staff, and, after the sermon, administered the sacrament of the Lord's-Supper to about twenty-five persons, among them the Lieutenant-Governor and family, Col. Ramsay, and some English soldiers. After service Col. Ramsay dined with us at the mission house. He remarked that we ought to have a mission at Pillibheet and at Gurhwall. To begin the latter he made an offer of $500, which, in a letter to Dr. Butler next morning, he raised to $1,500, adding $25 a month to sustain the proposed mission. Col. Ramsay is the commissioner of the district, and he has spent nearly thirty years in India.

On November 21st we start for Bareilly by way of Pillibheet, Dr. Butler and family in company. Col. Ramsay, attended by a number of natives, whom he had employed to work on the roads, overtook us as we were descending the mountain. Finding him on foot, I left the dhooley and walked several miles to enjoy his society. It may serve somewhat to illustrate the peculiarities of the country, to note some points of our conversation.

Just below the Jewteekot Mountain, the Colonel pointed to a stone in a ravine, where he says a tiger was accustomed to watch, until he had killed thirty persons, among them three sons of a widow. She, consulting a Fakir, was told that her sons were changed into tigers, but that if she could see the animal that devoured them she would receive them again in human shape. Accordingly she took her seat by the roadside and there sat day and night, month after month, watching for the beast, never asking alms, but being fed by the neighbors and the passing travelers. At length she was missed, and by her blood was traced to a rock, where her body was found partly eaten. The Colonel sent some hunters to the spot, who, hiding behind bushes, shot the tiger as he returned to his feast.

He pointed out another spot where a tiger fell upon a mail carrier, and seizing the mail-bags, sent his teeth through and through them, although they contained a large, well-bound army list. The dry meal, however, so discouraged the animal that he was easily driven from his prey. The Colonel spoke of a tiger which, to his knowledge, had killed fifty persons, many of them pilgrims on their way to the mountain shrines. The pilgrims having become scarce, he took his prey from a village. Three villages, with but one gun and one bullet, joined to pursue him. That bullet, fortunately, was lodged in the tiger's leg. By the wound it inflicted the animal was both disabled and made to mark his way with his blood. The pursuers coming up with him, assailed him with stones, until he turned upon them; in this way the conflict continued all day. When night came the villagers encamped, and next day they continued the pursuit.

On the morning of the third day they succeeded in stoning and beating him to death. Bears are a pretty good match for tigers. Buffaloes, singly, fall an easy prey to a tiger, but in a flock they form themselves into a living wedge, by which they support each other and crush the common foe. Leopards run from a tiger like cats from a dog. Elephants are trained to hunt them; they stun them with their trunks, and crush them beneath their feet. As we passed by a hut the owner told us that a tiger was killing his bullocks, and showed us the fresh horns of one that had been killed the night before. The

Government pays $1.50 for killing a bear, $2.50 for killing a leopard, and $5 for killing a tiger.

We reached Katgodam by 4, P. M., where we were detained getting ready the dhoolies until seven. The *dak* having been mislaid, we pursued a roundabout way during the night, so that at dawn we found ourselves at Baharny, where we extemporized breakfast, after which we received a friendly call from the native magistrate.

PILLIBHEET, BAREILLY, BUDAON.

Off now for Pillibheet, where we are met by Missionaries Waugh and Thomas. Here we have two and a half acres, namely, two in fee simple, and half an acre in perpetual lease—paying annual rent of $6—and a small, inferior house. This property cost $312; its present value is $269. Mr. Cawdell, once stationed here, left it on account of its unhealthiness. There are three English families here, and the joint magistrate tells us it is healthy nine months in the year. The city contains 39,000 people, and is well built. At the conference we sent a missionary to it.

On to Bareilly, estimated to contain 112,000 inhabitants, the most important station in Rohilcund. Our mission compound consists of 20

56-100 acres, worth $484. The mission house is very comfortable, newly whitewashed inside and out, and tastefully, though not extravagantly furnished. It is valued at $2,500. The Girls' Orphan School, of brick walls and cemented roof, is fifty feet by seventy-four, exclusive of veranda; value between $2,000 and $2,500. The Orphanage, worth $2,000, is inclosed by a wall, within which a few shrubs are planted, and more might be. Domestic outfit, $837; school requisites, $132; three native helpers' houses, $225; superintendent's house, $3,500. This is of brick walls and pucca roof. Itinerating outfit, $336; Bungalow rented to bank, $1,750; Orphans' graveyard, worth $38, with cheap inclosure, and wanting a bridge from the street, as the land is subject to inundation. It has eight little graves without monuments.

The chapel requisites are $180; school requisites, $41; itinerating requisites, $280; miscellaneous, $14. Connected with this mission is a printing establishment on a plot of ground containing five acres, worth $1,500. The house, used as an endowment of the press, is set down at $1,750. The printing-office is a koti sixty feet by forty-eight, value, $1,750. Press and stock, value, $3,250. Dwelling-house for the manager, a thatched bungalow, worth $2,000. There are outhouses reckoned in, which are occupied by native Christians and servants. Sixteen hands, of whom six are Christians, are employed in printing; half the time, however, in job work. The matter is in Hindee, or Urdu, or English. The Urdu is sometimes set in Roman, Arabic, and Persian characters. Among the books published are our hymn-book, catechism, and tracts, and the Psalms of David. Before I left Mrs. Thomas presented me with a beautiful Cashmere gown, the gift of the girls of the Orphanage—a memorial on which I place great value. The Orphanage is doing well in all its departments. I was deeply moved to see one little child in the matron's arms which had been literally dug out of the grave, where it had been placed by its unnatural parents.

We left Bareilly by carriage for Budaon; one of our horses was borrowed from a Mohammedan judge of the latter city. The distance is thirty miles; the road is tolerable to the Ramgunga, intolerable over the deep sands in the vicinity of that stream, and excellent beyond, where it is a broad metaled highway, made by the British before the mutiny. Along the road many of the fields are well cultivated, but there is a great deal of waste land adorned by peacocks, and infested by jackals and wolves. Mr.

Scott tells me that three old persons and two children were carried off lately from Budaon by wolves. The natives are not allowed to bear arms without a license, and as this can not be obtained without some reputation, or retained without tax, the chief weapons of defense are clubs.

The deeds of our property at Budaon are satisfactory. The mission premises are well situated, half a mile from the city, on three acres of ground. The dwelling-house contains eight rooms, and is worth $1,600. The church is sixty feet by thirty, worth $565; both have pucca roofs. Native helper's house worth $75; Zyat, $69; Chapel requisites, $30; school requisites, $63; itinerating requisites, $110; miscellaneous property, $5. The ground is subject to an annual rent of $20.

Every Sabbath there is preaching in the native language, a Sabbath-school, and a Bible class for females. On Tuesday, English service, class-meeting, Bible class. Every week a prayer-meeting is held. Bazaar preaching is according to circumstances, generally every third day. During my stay we had an extra meeting, at which I addressed the people and administered the Lord's-Supper, and Mr. Scott preached in the native tongue. We have here two native preachers, three school-teachers, forty native hearers at Sabbath service, twenty Sabbath-school scholars, twelve Church members, three probationers, ninety-two pupils, of whom eighty are boys and twelve girls. The members, with a single exception, are *independent of the mission*, and all suffer social disability and other inconveniences for their faith. The schools were carefully inspected. There is one in the church, with an average attendance of thirty pupils, having two teachers, a Hindoo and a Mohammedan; another in the bazaar, average attendance twenty, one teacher, a Hindoo and an inquirer. While I was at the mission a Mohammedan called on the missionary, and expressed deep concern for his soul.

On our return journey to Bareilly we broke down on the sands near the Ramgunga, walked a mile or two, got on a bullock hackery, and thus rode until we came to our last station. We arrived at Bareilly in the evening; next day drove out to cantonments, where brethren are putting up a chapel, to cost $150, and to be used both for church and school. Returning, we passed the spot where, in the mutiny, the British officers were shot down in endeavoring to escape. Prudently, before this event, Dr. Butler's family had started for the hills. The cantonments, officers' and Government quarters, are all admirable. There is good English society here. The city has the best bazaar and serai I have seen in India; the former is three miles long, substantial and ornamented. There are here Government hospitals, a lunatic asylum, and a prison, with two thousand prisoners.

Sabbath, we had Hindoostani preaching by a native—Joel—and the sacrament of the Lord's-Supper. When Dr. Butler first came here he borrowed Joel from the Presbyterian Mission at Allahabad, but he has never returned him, and as Joel is a thorough Methodist, the lenders probably do not want him. He is well informed, and speaks with dignity, fluency, and force, and, the missionaries add, with *unction*. He has a young wife and four children, and lives in a mud cottage, with a kitchen at one end, a study at the other, and a dining-room between. Behind his house is an inclosure, walled and protected by tiles, where the family sit and sleep. There is another native preacher here—William—who lives within the Orphanage inclosure, in a similar habitation to Joel's. Each has a small library. Joel has Benson's Commentary, William has Clarke's. It is interesting to see the children at meals. They sit in rows upon the ground, each having a metallic plate, but neither spoon, knife, nor fork. After prayer they arise, one row after another, go to a large kettle, where, having had their platters filled, they return and reseat themselves. The kettle contains a mixture of rice and dahl, and ghee or melted butter. A matron at another kettle dispenses to such as desire it a small quantity of catsup. After all have received supplies and reseated themselves, a blessing is asked, and the company depart by sixes or sevens to their respective rooms, where, seated on the floor, they enjoy their repast. Twice a week the children are allowed meat. On Sabbath afternoon we had English service. I preached, and afterward administered the sacrament to thirty or forty persons, some white. The latter came first. A gentleman and his wife, who were Baptists, partook seated.

SHAHJEHANPORE, SEETAPORE, AND GONDAH.

In the dhooley for Shahjehanpore, fifty miles distant, when within thirteen miles of the place, we were met by brother Brown with horses, on which we gallop to the Gurra, where, on the opposite bank, Dr. Johnson is in waiting with a buggy. At this station, on Sabbath, Mr. Brown preaches in Hindoostani in the morning, holds Sunday-school in the afternoon, and class-meeting in the evening. Every Wednesday is prayer-meeting; every Sabbath, and four times a week besides, bazaar preaching. The number of members is twenty-one; of probationers, five. There is one native preacher, Rev. H. M. Daniel, who understands Ordu, Persian, Sanscrit, Arabic, Hebrew, Latin, Greek, and English. He has twelve hundred acres of land, which he visits occasionally, preaching to his tenants. About half the members here belong to the Orphanage; the rest are independent of the mission. Just across the river stands Lodipoor, which Major Gowan purchased for us at an expense of $2,500. There are five acres of ground in connection with it, and twenty-three acres in addition held on perpetual lease at $70 a year. Mr. Brown's school is in a large house, formerly the mansion of a Nawab, now owned by a sugar company, which gives the school accommodation at $5 a month. The pupils enrolled are one hundred and fifteen, of which there is an average attendance of ninety. There are four teachers, all Mussulmans. The school is opened with prayer, and the Scriptures are read every morning. The smaller children are examined in the catechism, and all are required to attend preaching every Sabbath. In the city, near the *Chowk*, a site has been purchased for a *Zyat*, where the missionary may hold conversation, sell books, and preach the Gospel. The population of the city is 75,000, chiefly Mohammedans. Our boys' Orphanage is badly located, because in cantonments, which subjects it to the control of the military authorities, and because close by the soldiers' bazaar, which is infested by bad characters. In the institution, the buildings of which are tolerably good, we have seventy-seven boys and four teachers, besides monitors. Rev. Mr. Daniel, native, is head-master. Arithmetic, Geography, Ordu, Persian, English, Hindee, and Sanscrit are taught. The Biblical instruction is satisfactory, the writing of the pupils is good, and their drawing excellent; but in English grammar and arithmetic the examination was not very creditable. The Orphanage is to be transferred to the property purchased for the purpose by Major Gowan.

The property belonging to the station is as follows: Ten acres in cantonments, cost nothing; rent, $1 a month. On this stands a double house, worth, including wells, native preacher's house, etc., $4,000; a small building, $750; church, $50; native helper's house, $250; furniture for church and school, $128; itinerating and miscellaneous requisites, $23; Orphanage property at Lodipoor, $2,525; Orphanage buildings, $2,240; school-house money, $2,750; school furniture, $139; domestic, $288.

As we left Shahjehanpore the boys drew up in a line on each side of the dhooley and sung, under the direction of Mrs. Johnson, "I want to be an angel" and "There is a happy land." The sound of these familiar lines, in my native tongue, and in well-known strains, coming from Hindoo voices, and in a strange land, reminded me of home far away, and my better home above, in most overcoming modes.

In the morning we extemporize breakfast by the roadside. At eleven o'clock we reach Luckimpore, where we are received with great cordiality by the commissioner, Mr. Kavanaugh, who rents our mission-house here. This city has 5,000 inhabitants, and is improving. A large column marks the center of a new town, which the commissioner is encouraging the natives to build. Our property is well situated, and commands extensive and delightful views. It contains ten acres, on which stands a dwelling-house of six large rooms and seven small ones. It is a bungalow, sixty feet by eighty, with tile roof and pucca foundation, and is worth $1,750; but the roof needs repairing, which will cost $400. The church is small and decaying, and is worth only what the material in it will bring. We have a native helper's house, worth $50; other property, $75. Our missionaries forsook the place, perhaps not wisely, but the English residents are anxious for their return. Near by is Allegunj, which has 10,000 people; within three miles is Keri, and within four a range of large land grants made to English gentlemen who were useful during the mutiny. We leave for Seetapore on an elephant, in company with Dr. B. and Mr. Gracey. At Hirgauo, fifteen miles off, we are set down at midnight by the roadside, and after refreshment, prepared under a tree by starlight, we take the dhooley for Seetapore, where Mrs. Gracy and Mrs. Waugh were waiting for us at table. Our property here consists of nine and a half acres; a dwelling-house, fifty-four feet by seventy-four, containing four large rooms and seven small ones. Its walls are cutcha, with pucca foundations and capping; its value is $2,000. We have also a native preacher's house, $75; and other property worth $187. The land rent which we pay is $18 per annum.

This station, with which Luckimpore is connected, has four exhorters, four school-teachers, seven male members and seven female, two probationers, one class-meeting, at which the average attendance is eight, an average native Sabbath congregation of twenty, two schools with eighty male and three female scholars, and an English Sabbath congregation of twenty-five persons.. Brothers Gracey and Jackson live very comfortably. Nearly all our missionaries have pianos. Mrs. Jackson has also a sewing-machine. Seetapore has 6,000 inhabitants; Khairabad, five miles off, has 20,000. We are now in Oude, of which the latter is the third city in importance. It contains celebrated tombs and mosques. Here we have a school of which a native has charge. The Government wishes us to have a large school here, and would pay half the expenses, both of buildings and teachers, including a missionary, who ought to superintend it. At our school here a Mohammedan was formerly employed as master, under promise that he would teach the Bible and catechise the children; but as he omitted all allusion to the Trinity, and other things distinctive of Christianity, he was discharged. On leaving, he took all the Mussulman children with him. At first we did not charge for tuition, and on requiring a fee, the number of children diminished from forty-five to thirty-seven, but they are increasing now. The head-master is a merely nominal one. The English barracks in Seetapore, which is a military station, are very good, and even ornamental; but those for the native soldiery are low mud huts.

We had an interesting meeting here in Mr. G.'s parlor. The congregation was partly of soldiers, partly of native citizens. I opened with singing and prayer, and a discourse to the English, to whom I administered the Lord's-Supper. I then delivered a discourse to the Hindoos, which, I am told, was interpreted beautifully by the head teacher of the Government College in this city, a native, who was converted under the ministry of Dr. Duff.

We left Seetapore by dhooley at 4 o'clock, P. M., and traveled incessantly until ten o'clock at night of the following day before we reached Gondah—ninety miles—passing through Byram Ghat and Secrora. Until we reached the latter place the road was bad, and the sands near the Goggra were exceedingly heavy. Thence we had a *pucca* road. We were entertained very kindly by the magistrate, Mr. Knighton, an alumnus of Dublin University. He had retired when we arrived, but arose and insisted on giving us a warm supper. In the vicinity lives the Maharajah of Bulrampoor, a man of liberal principles and liberal spirit, who keeps five hundred soldiers just to play soldiering and add to his dignity. Gondah has 8,000 people, and was formerly a military station, though now it has but a few English families. The district of which it is the head is three hundred miles long, and numbers a million inhabitants. Its chief towns are Gondah, Bulrampore, 5,000; Uttroulah, 6,000; Shahpore, 7,000; Nawalying, 6,000; Toolesepoor, 10,000; Purruspoor, 8,000; Murkipore, 10,000; Sallgunj, 10,000. The district is chiefly agricultural. The Maharajah of Bulrampoor and the Rajahs of Singa Chunda, Purruspoor, Murkipoor, and Maharajah Mann Sing are the chief landholders. There are in the city many Shiwallahs built by wealthy families, either to the goddess of fortune—Lakshim—or the goddess of health, some of which are evidently new. In them, families to which they belong pay their regular devotions. Dr. Butler preached on Sabbath morning a very appropriate sermon in the parlor of Mr. Knighton, to a company of eight or ten persons, mostly English-speaking natives in the employ of Government. At this city, on an island in a lake made artificially about three hundred years ago, is a temple. The lake, eight feet deep, was made by excavating for the island. From its waters to the temple platform the island is fronted by solid masonry, stone steps being placed at each end. The worshipers cross in canoes hewed out of the trunk of the seisam-tree. The temple is built over the tomb of a Brahmin, who was a Rishi and the founder of a new order. Here he lived and died, thus consecrating the spot; and here priests minister, and also train disciples. Around the lake are many tombs, some quite expensive, and much like Mohammedan sepulchers. They are a curiosity, as the Hindoos generally burn their dead. I could not leave that million of people without resolving to send them a missionary.

FYZABAD, ROY BAREILLY, LUCKNOW.

On we go to Fyzabad, which we reach in the morning, and where we are entertained by the assistant magistrate, Mr. Smith, who drove us round the city, the second in Oude, and through the neighboring city, Ajoudia, the most remarkable place in Northern India. It is supposed by Buchanan to have been founded 1366 B. C., and is said by some native authorities to have been, at one time, two hundred miles long. Its antiquity is not, however, its chief charm. It contains the fort of Hanuman, in honor of the fabulous monkey god, which has an annual revenue of $25,000 settled on it by Sujah ud Dowlah. Here, too, is the ruined fort of Rama, hero of the Ramayana. Our approach to the temple of Hanuman is through a busy market, in which the principal thing sold is flowers for offerings. We ascend the temple by a long flight of stone steps, flanked by living monkeys. It is a college or theological seminary, endowed with lands, and attended by four hundred priests, who are monks under the control of a superior, said to be one hundred years old. He was seated on a platform besmeared with the symbols of his god, while a young priest was rubbing him to revive him. In a veranda the novices are attentively and reverently hearing the sacred books read and expounded.

When a Rajah builds a temple he sends hither for a priest. The number in this community is large. When it is in need of funds it sends out a priest to receive alms or levy tax. The offerings are many and costly. The idol is a miserable-looking object, under a gold canopy, and having a crown of pearls, which on special occasions are replaced by diamonds. One of the latter was presented by Maharajah Mann Sing, and is said to be next to the Kohinoor. Many of the priests wear long hair plaited and twisted round the head in form of a cap. One said that his hair had not been cut in nine years. Entering the court-yard, we saw a large elephant marked as a worshiper. He belonged to the temple, and was chained by his forefeet. We were advised to beware of him.

On we go to a temple just built by a Rajah at a cost of $200,000. The painting is fresh, and better than we have elsewhere seen in India. Many gods are represented on the wall, such as the Triad, earth, sun, fire, water. The moon is depicted as a human form surrounded by twenty-seven rivers. The most noticeable image is that of a man out of whose head and back seven serpents are growing. The priest said, "That is the supreme god," and supposing we did not apprehend him, he added, "Jesus Christ." We noticed a new shiwallah near by. On we go to the Ghat. Here worshipers are bathing in the Goggra. A priest being informed who we were, cried out, "I am a priest of the Hindoos; I teach them; they do as I bid them." He had just been feeding an enormous monkey. We pass now to see the most sacred spot in India, Ram's birthplace. It is marked by a simple broad platform of pucca work, on which rest the floral offerings of the faithful. When the Mohammedans took possession of the place they transformed the adjacent temple into a mosque. The Hindoos, after a dreadful fight, retook the place, but could not retain it until the British gave it to them. They have not yet had courage to take down the mosque, which, however, is separated from the sacred spot by a stone wall. Fyzabad has 75,000 people, and is increasing. It is the seat of considerable trade and manufactures. The hospital is a noble structure, which was built by a resident Rajah at a cost of $25,000. It is under the care of Dr. Wishaw and native subordinates. The patients were nearly all outside in the sun, without protection even for the head; many of them were from the hills. Most of this class had goiter, which is treated successfully with binoxide of mercury applied externally.

On our way through the city we are delayed by elephants, who take up the road and move slowly. Fyzabad is in our bounds, and ought to have been occupied by us; but the Church Missionary Society has anticipated us, not kindly.

Our next journey is to Roy Bareilly, distant eighty miles, or seven stations, which we reach after twenty-one hours' travel. We breakfast by the roadside near Mahangunj. On arriving at brother Wilson's we at once set out for the city, calling on the way upon Major Orr, the commissioner. He was once in the service of the king of Oude, but during the mutiny he did good service on the staff of Sir James Outram. The district is agricultural. The land is owned by Talookdars, of whom the Government requires half the produce of the land, besides half a dollar per cent. for roads, and another for schools. As

Government oppresses the Talookdars, so they, in turn, oppress the ryots.

Our station has, first, a house in cantonment, value, $350, to be used in the new building; second, three acres of land, near the city, on which we pay a yearly rent of $16. On this is a native helper's house, value, $175. Third, church and school furniture, itinerating apparatus, etc., $26. We are building a new house to cost $550. This station was founded March, 1864. Its staff is the missionary and his wife and two exhorters. We have a native congregation, with an average attendance of ten, and we already number three members and three probationers. The services are, Sabbath morning, preaching in the church, bazaar preaching daily, except Tuesdays and Saturdays, generally in two places at the same time; class-meeting every Tuesday; prayer-meeting every Thursday. Our native members are dependent on the mission; namely, native helpers and the moonshi. There are two out-stations.

Our next journey is to Lucknow, by dhooley; but when within twelve miles of the city we meet with a dog-cart sent out for us. We reach Mr. Judd's at six o'clock, having enjoyed, on the way, a fine view of the civil and military lines, the royal palace and gardens, and been deeply impressed with the Oriental appearance of the city, and its remains of former grandeur.

Next day is Conference. Before this, however, a committee waited upon me to read a memorial protest, setting forth that the Conference about to be formed would not have the usual rights of such a body, answering certain real or imaginary arguments for the restrictions under which it was to be placed, and finally asking that these be removed; a document which will, doubtless, receive respectful consideration at the General Conference. The session was remarkably harmonious. Natives were admitted and ordained upon an equality with their brethren from America. There was some misgiving in regard to this policy, but I feel certain that it is right. The preachers admitted are well qualified, and could pass a satisfactory examination in any of our Conferences. To exclude them, or put them under any disability on account of color, would be at once a blunder and a sin.

In Hosinabad, a part of Lucknow, we have five acres, on which are two dwelling-houses, one 66 by 69 feet, containing five large rooms and ten small ones, value, $2,850; the other, 45 by 73 feet, having ten rooms, value, $2,400. Both are pucca.

In this estimate we include native helpers'

houses, gates, walls, and wells. We have also a school-house in the bazaar. It is 76 by 90 feet, containing eight rooms and a basement with six. It stands on a quarter of an acre, free of rent, value, $3,000. We have a school-house and dwelling at Sadatgunj, the former worth $250, the latter $300. In the east part of the city we have a residence and church worth $3,000; in Hosinabad we have a graveyard in which are the graves of Downey and others. This is estimated at $50. Add church and school furniture and itinerating facilities, $630, and we have a total of $12,466 in this station.

To the property of the mission must be added the outfits of the treasurer, secretary, and sanitarium, $110. The station of Lucknow has one native preacher, one exhorter, eight school-teachers, an average native congregation of thirty persons, a Sunday-school of fifty-five pupils, a native church of eleven adult members and eight probationers, a class-meeting, with an average attendance of twelve members, a day-school of one hundred and fifty-seven pupils, and an average daily attendance of one hundred and thirty. We had an English congregation, but it passed into the hands of the Wesleyans. They, however, returned the church to us during my visit. Our school is in competent hands.

What Julian said of Damascus we may say of Lucknow: "Surpassing every [Indian] city both in the beauty of its temples and the magnitude of its shrines, as well as the timeliness of its seasons, the limpidness of its fountains," if not the volume of its waters, and the richness of its soil.

The plain statement of facts and estimates given in these papers is deemed due both to the missions and the Church. The facts may at first sight seem uninteresting, but they throw light upon the condition and character of the country. The estimates, it should be borne in mind, are upon a gold basis, and the property having been built in a land where wages are exceedingly low, is far superior to what the mere figures might indicate.

On the whole, it will be seen that our India missions deserve the confidence of the Church, and the more fully they are understood the more strong will that confidence be. No one could have been a more pleasant companion than Dr. Butler. Had I been a son he could not have treated me with more kindness.

VI.

INDIA CONFERENCE.

THE following is the address which I delivered at the opening of the first session of the India Mission Annual Conference:

Before we proceed to organize I beg to submit a few remarks which our unusual circumstances suggest.

I come from your native land, bearing from your brethren greeting and love. The country and Church which sent you hither remember you. Identified as you are with the cause of God in this great and populous peninsula, it is natural that we should bear you up in our prayers. Nor are we unmindful of your trials. It is no small matter to bid farewell to home and native lands; to settle in a climate which is pretty sure to disturb our health, if it do not abridge our life; to rear our children under influences and institutions which we disapprove, and forfeit for them literary, social, and political privileges, to which, in our own land, they would have fallen heirs; to move amid foes, and to be regarded as intruders. It is a still greater trial, far from a land of Sabbath bells, separated from the watch-care of the Church, and deprived of the communion of the saints, to be subjected, through every sense, to pagan influences. He who moves amid the temples of idolatry moves in a great moral pest-house. Nothing but open, perpetual, prayerful resistance to the forces that play upon him can keep him safe. The human mind, unsustained by grace, gravitates to religious error. The Mohammedans entered India enemies both to idolatry and caste, but instead of destroying them they gradually adopted them. Christianity, too, on its first introduction into this land, compromised its principles. Even the primitive Church, when she relaxed her war upon idolatry, became polluted by it.

You do not, however, ask our sympathy. Penetrated with your high calling, you are ready to deny yourselves, endure afflictions, make full proof of your ministry, and through perils either by sea or land, by robbers or false brethren, remain unmoved; willing, if need be, to die for the Lord Jesus, and when you do, to commend to your children the battle you fought, committing them confidently to the care of your Father, and their Father, to whom you ascend through the grace of his Son.

We know, indeed, that no lower standard is set before us. We, too, have learned to bear the reproach of Christ. But we discern that in you the Christian conflict is more than ordinarily severe, and we inquire what more can we do for you, what new comforts, auxiliaries, and supports can we send you? Engaged as we are in a war for the national life, against an unprovoked, wanton, and wicked rebellion—I say unprovoked, for no encroachment on the rights of the South was either inflicted or threatened; wanton, for the insurgents controlled all branches of the Government when they rebelled, and might have held them to this day; wicked, for what more so than to sever States

> "Which mutual league,
> United thoughts and counsels, equal hope
> And hazard in all glorious enterprises,"

had joined, and plunged them into war, even to the verge of ruin? Yet we have never once thought of withholding support from our missions, or even slacking the combat which we carry on through the earth against the powers of darkness. Saying this, we say much, for our war is one of awful magnitude, counting its battles by the hundred, its dead and wounded by the million, and its expenditures by figures like those in which we compute the celestial spaces. Yet we say to you, stand to your post; we will not only supply but re-enforce you. You can not do our Church justice without considering that she has poured out more blood and suffered more losses for her country than any other.

> "Many a bleeding father hath borne his valiant sons
> In coffins from the field."

The tears of orphans, and the sighs of widows, and the lamentations of weeping Rachels that will not be comforted, make the whole Church like a funeral procession. But I need not tell *you*, for the crape is upon you also. Do you ask why this expenditure of life? Because there are things dearer than life. The Church regards the war, terrible as it is, as, on the part of the Government, unavoidable and righteous, arising out of the existence in some of the States of an institution incompatible alike with the genius of our republic, the spirit of our age, and the principles of our religion; an institution toward which, in former days, she was tolerant and hopeful, but which she has now placed under unequivocal ban. Seeing that law, liberty, and light are on one side of this conflict, and rebellion, slavery, and darkness on the other, we can but hope concerning the issue. Men, indeed, tell us that reunion is impossible, as if our adversary had

> "The unconquerable will
> And study of revenge, immortal hate
> And courage never to submit or yield."

Such spirit is not found outside of hell; least of all, among those who bow at the altar of Jesus. While

> "Devil with devil damned firm concord holds,
> Shall States of creatures rational, though under hope
> Of heavenly grace, forever disagree?"

and while earth and heaven cry peace,

> "Yet live in hatred, enmity, and strife,
> Among themselves, and levy cruel wars,
> Wasting the earth each other to destroy;"

as if the Union had not foes enough besides,

> "That day and night for its destruction wait."

Should the war end as we anticipate, it will leave us a stronger Government, a more homogeneous people, and a higher civilization, while it removes the only motive for disunion.

Of the noble warriors that have fallen in the conflict on both sides, we say, let loving friends give them honorable graves; but of slavery, as the poet says of Tamora,

> "No funeral rite, nor man in mournful weeds,
> No mournful bell shall ring her burial;
> But throw her forth to beasts and birds of prey.
> Her life was beastlike, and devoid of pity;
> And, being so, shall have like want of pity."

Then shall our land be the hope and refuge equally of every tribe, kindred, tongue, and color. At such a consummation men might utter praise, and angels halleluiahs; none more so than missionaries. When we come proclaiming the fatherhood of God and the brotherhood of man, and those two precepts founded on them, upon which hang both the law and the prophets, the heathen might say, "Go back; preach them to your own people first." A native newspaper has just admonished us not to boast of the results of Christianity, since American Christianity sanctions slavery. The United States, planted between the Atlantic and the Pacific, as if to throw her influence over both, given to the best races, unequaled in the products of her soil and treasures of her mountains, unembarrassed by the political complications and institutions of the Old World, and free from temptation to conquer the distant lands, seems intended to be the great missionary nation. Is it no advantage to say, "We own no provinces, we desire none; we exercise no authority over you, and seek no gain of you; all we seek is to bring you to Christ?"

Our difficulties in spreading the Gospel in this land are great, yet in all of them we find grounds of encouragement. One of the greatest difficulties arises from a deep conviction in the minds of the natives that strangers in propagating their religion have some selfish end in view. While our national relations relieve us in great measure from this imputation, it is hoped that our neat, though inexpensive homes, our healthful but frugal tables, our kind consideration of the poor, and our whole life and conversation, will convince the natives that not *personal* interest but the love of Christ constraineth us. Indeed, if this be in us it will be known, for the world is a "palace full of tongues, and eyes, and ears," each thrilling with deep and scrutinizing intelligence.

Another difficulty lies in the fact that Christians who preceded us have depreciated their religion. An emperor of Japan being asked what was the religion of the Dutch, replied, "They are merchants;" and when the question was asked again, answered, "Merchants; merchants have no religion but to make money." And what of the English? It is not the whole truth to say, as Lord Bentinck did, that the fundamental maxim of British rule is strict neutrality; or as Lord Macaulay, "We abstain from giving any encouragement to those engaged in the work of converting the natives to Christianity;" or as Lord Ellenborough, "We withhold the aid of the Government from schools with which missionaries are connected." The East India Company withheld *private* aid. Lord Landsdowne declared that if Lord Canning had subscribed to a Missionary Society he ought to be removed. They neglected religion themselves. For fifty years they had no place of worship. For two hundred years they sought to prevent attempts to convert the natives. Down to 1813 they refused all missionaries passage in their ships, denied them permission to land, and if they effected a landing drove them from their shores. In 1814 they debarred native Christians from offices of respectability. Nor was this negative support of idolatry all. They repaired pagodas by taxing pilgrims, expended large sums at the request of priests for the support of heathen and Mohammedan worship, administered revenues in connection with pagan temples, and even took a share in heathen festivals.

The Company, we grant, advanced the intelligence, developed the resources, and diminished the crime of the country; and after it allowed the Christian faith to enlighten the native mind, it drew a distinction between morality and religion, and forbade the destruction of human life in heathen ceremonies, as under other circumstances; but its whole course was characterized by a proud bearing, an insatiable avarice, and an all-devouring encroachment. The personal influence of the English rulers did not counteract their political course. While they did not practice polygamy, many of them did worse. The natives therefore thought either that we despised our own religion, or that, concealing our designs, we intended to convert them to it by a trick, such as greasing cartridges; a thought which never could have entered their minds had they understood our faith. Rebellion, instead of conversion, was the natural result.

In suppressing it martial law was proclaimed, the property of rebels confiscated, searches and seizures made without warrant, suspected persons hung, and Sepoys blown from guns. We do not say all this was unnecessary, though we may be allowed a parenthesis in which to remark that the people who put down an insurrection in this way should not reproach another for seeking to put down a more formidable revolt by means less severe; and to add, what is more to our purpose, that this bloody process had a temporary tendency to hinder the spread among the conquered of the religion of the conquerors. Horrible as it was, however, it was hardly to be deplored, since it seems to have settled the question of the permanence of European civilization and Christian faith in this peninsula, and to have placed the country under the direct government of a Christian sovereign of distinguished virtues, whose present viceroy and subordinate governors are worthy representatives of such a queen. Our Articles of Religion require us not only to be subject to the supreme civil authority, but to use all laudable means to secure obedience to the powers that be. Happy are we that our civil duty is our personal pleasure. Under the flag whose protection we accept, we may see every interest of the country, political, commercial, and religious, steadily and rapidly advancing, and the fabled reign of Tisso realized: precious metals and gems buried in the earth rising to the surface, treasures sunk in the sea appearing on the shore, and bamboos rearing themselves laden with richest flowers, quadrupeds, and fruits. The providence of God moves in

> "Mazes intricate,
> Eccentric, intervolved, yet regular
> Then most, when most irregular they seem;
> And in their motions harmony divine
> So smooths her charming tones, that God's own ear
> Listens delighted;"

while even the wrath of man praises him.

Formerly, Indian patriotism may have suggested the expulsion of the Christian faith; now it suggests its adoption. For as soon as India shall accept the religion of Christ and the civilization which grows out of it, England will voluntarily retire from her shores. Should she do so before she would commit a great crime, and India suffer a great misfortune.

But greater difficulties confront us. Caste stereotypes humanity, and bids defiance to any force to break up its plates. It makes him who becomes a Christian an outcast; it deprives him of the advantages of association, of the profits of business, of all the sweet charities of father, son, brother, and often even of wife and child. It drives him from men to dwell among beasts. It enters not only into the social but the national life. It can not be defied without a ripeness for martyrdom. None can appreciate it but such as come in contact with it. Originating with the priesthood, and designed to perpetuate their power, it is guarded by them with a sleepless eye. Yet it is nevertheless doomed. There is a revolution which it can not resist, a revolution without pomp, or retinue, or violence, or corrupting gold; it is the revolution of ideas. Every movement of the pen over the paper, or the electric stream over the wires, or of the school-house door upon its hinges, or of the fire-breathing horse over his iron track, marks its progress. Caste is inconsistent with principles which are self-evident and rights which are inalienable. All men are naturally free and equal, and ought to be allowed life, liberty, and the pursuit of happiness, unembarrassed by hinderances which the providence of God does not impose, and unaided by distinctions which merit or its consequences do not confer.

Below caste lie greater difficulties: superstition, bigotry, idolatry. Among minds unaccustomed to patient and vigorous thought, events which are merely connected by accidental association are often viewed in the relation of cause and effect. Hence unlucky days, absurd remedies for disease, and omens of good and evil. Among those unacquainted with natural sciences and unguided by a divine revelation, nothing is more easy than to attribute unusual events to supernatural powers. From this it is a slight step to body forth and name these images of the mind, and thus people heaven and earth with supernal and infernal divinities. Then we must pour forth our gratitude to the one and appease the malignity of the other. Hence oblations and sacrifices. These require a priesthood; and a profane priesthood once created will secure its permanence and enlarge its power by keeping the people in ignorance. Even could we suppose men enlightened without revelation the same result might be expected. The human heart is made to reverence something. It is to the credit of India that she reasoned herself up to the most sublime theology, and to her shame that she reasoned herself down to the lowest depths of idolatry. She said, Let us worship Brahma, the greatest. Where shall we find it? Not in the stream that fertilizes the land, nor the sun which warms it, for the parts are not so great as the whole. Shall it then be the universe? But what were the universe without eyes to see its beauty, ears to catch its harmony, and hearts to enjoy its bounty? Spirit is greater than matter. Let *it* then be greatest. But *what* spirit? The spirit of man is greater than that of beasts. Shall man then worship his own spirit? If so, in what mood? for it has various moods. The spirit awake is impressed and modified by material objects. The spirit dreaming, which sees only spiritual objects, must be greater than the spirit waking. But this is moved to laughter or to weeping, and is after all conscious of the unreal nature of its scenes. Is not the spirit in repose, unagitated by passion or motion, greater than either the waking or dreaming one? But this is an unconscious state; there must be something greater: the Spirit which created it and all other things, the Spirit of the universe.

But this is infinite, invisible, intangible, and therefore can not be comprehended. But his functions can—creation, preservation, destruction; hence Brahma, Vishnu, Siva. But these are abstractions. The masses said to the philosophers, We can not love what we can not understand, and we will not worship what we can not love. We will have gods nearer and warmer. In looking for a god they found a man. Rama had extraordinary virtues. They said, "Here is one greater than human, he must be a god." When he dies he is transported in imagination to the heavens. In process of time it is found easy, among a credulous people, without contemporaneous literature or knowledge of the laws of evidence, to enlarge his powers and exaggerate his virtues by myths. One god having been introduced into the Pantheon others follow. Moreover, if that which brings deliverance or pleasure is to be deified, then the stream which waters and the sun which enlightens the land, and the rock which throws its shadow over the weary path, may be worshiped, and that which affords the greatest pleasure with the least trouble may be worshiped most. Thus gods are multiplied until they number three hundred and thirty-three millions. The character ascribed to them and the devotions devised for them, coming from the human heart, where lurk evil thoughts, murders, adulteries, etc., must be corrupting and degrading. No wonder that at length thieves, and drunkards, and adulterers, and beasts become gods, and riot and lasciviousness crown the ceremonies of the sanctuary. When men come to model heaven,

> "How they wield
> The mighty frame; how build, unbuild, contrive
> To save appearances; how gird the sphere
> With centric and eccentric scribbled o'er,
> Cycle and epicycle, orb in orb;"

yet every progress of thought "making confusion worse confounded." Indian idolatry has touched bottom. As I stood in the holy city Benares, every sense disgusted, and every feeling merged in indignation, contemplating the stupidity, the odiousness, the obscenity, the discord, the beastliness of that center of pagan worship, I thought, Surely it can get no lower without opening the mouth of hell. I exclaimed, within myself, "Almighty God! to what depths of darkness and depravity are thy rational creatures capable of descending, when they turn away from the revelation of love and mercy!" As I looked upon a Fakir seated by the Ganges, naked, haggard, worn to a skeleton, and covered with ashes, I thought I knew what it is to be damned.

The human mind having reached its limit of false theology must recoil. Hindooism is like a building whose walls are honeycombed, and whose rafters are tunneled by ants. That a system so monstrous has stood so long, we can easily comprehend. The power of the priesthood has been cemented for ages; the religion is inwoven with the national life and social habits of the people. The distinctions transmitted through ages, the festivals to which the people are used, the arts and manufactures, the literature and science in which they excel, the laws and courts which kindle their bosoms with a patriot's flame; all, it is feared, must fall with the national faith. Moreover, all religion has a foundation in truth; namely, that the universe is under the guidance of supernatural powers. And the more venerable the truth, the more permanent the error grafted upon it. The god that is first associated with our sacred thoughts, to which we lift up infant hands, and which we bless with lips fresh from a mother's breast, can not be easily displaced from the heart. We know how superstition lingers even in Christian lands and philosophic minds. Yet even this should not discourage us, but rather teach us the proper modes of assault.

Harmless as doves, let us be wise as serpents.

In pouring contempt upon the Puranas, and exposing the institutes of Menu, we may point Hindoos to their more venerable and pure theology. The Vedas afford us a stand-point. The nation that was among the earliest to syllogize and geometrize, and to reason up to the sublimest heights of metaphysics, can be shamed out of that idolatry which so degrades and stupefies man, and misrepresents, and abuses, and slanders God; substituting blocks and beasts for Him who makes the clouds his chariot, the thunder his voice, the earth his footstool, and the heaven his throne. Then there are traditions which we may press into our service. The incarnation is admitted by Hindoos; we have only to identify Christ with it. I envy the brother to be stationed at Sumbul. Beneath that temple guarded and venerated as the cradle of an incarnate God, who is to come as a Savior of mankind, I would preach as Paul did at the altar of the unknown God. I envy, too, those who preach to intelligent Mohammedans, the privilege of quoting the testimony of the Koran to the Law, the Prophets, and the Evangel. We must teach the Natural Sciences, and show how the universe is governed by fixed laws devised by an infinite and eternal mind, who, nevertheless, answers prayer according to his promise, not perhaps by altering physical laws, but by adjustments of humanity to them through the higher laws of the spiritual world. Thus men will learn to dread only sin, and seek relief only in prayer to our Heavenly Father, through Jesus Christ, his Son! We must teach the young, both because of the ease with which impressions are made upon their minds, and because of the durability of such impressions, which are inwoven with the very texture of the soul. If you would write your words in a book; if you would cut them on the lead with stylet of iron; if you would drive them with chisel and mallet into the rock; if you would send them down the ages, and centuries, and millenniums, ay, into eternity, write upon the *young* soul. The knowledge of late years seems to crumble off in the storms of time, leaving the impressions of the sweet period of prime. How often do we see the Ceylonese or Hindoo convert relapse in age or sickness! According to Lucian, the name Ptolemy was inscribed on the Pharos—that proud monument of Alexandria. But the artist, to secure the glory of the work, cut his own name in the stone, and the monarch's in the stucco that covered it; so that in process of time the stucco falling, revealed the record of the architect. In teaching youth, beware whom you employ. Remember the power of a master, *ipse dixit.* I have no faith in heathen teachers. The Brahmin teaching the Bible is the Greek bearing gifts to Troy. You could teach the Koran so that no pupil would believe it. In estimating your work, men may count your one hundred and sixty-four converts. Look rather to your thirteen hundred and twenty-two scholars. A few years will reduce the former to zero, but multiply the latter by five. Especially may we regard with hope the education of females. Inferior, ignorant as the Hindoo mother may be, her influence is well-nigh irresistible. She needs but breathe her faith upon her little one, and though her lord may instruct, and argue, and confound, she knows, alas! too well how to intermix grateful digressions,

> "And solve high dispute
> With conjugal caresses."

From her lips flow sweeter things than words. Even British officers have painted themselves and danced to idols, to please woman less than wife. Satan needed not to trouble himself about Adam after he had captured Eve. Nor will India be retaken from him until we imitate his tactics, and attack it at that side which, though strongest for our defense, is weakest to our assault; for woman is oppressed and depressed by idolatry. If she lost Paradise by her desire of knowledge, may she not be induced to regain it by tasting the same inviting fruit?

Our greatest difficulty arises from the opposition of our enemies, and our apparent want of success. Temples are multiplying, priests are active, emissaries of error are abroad, tracts are distributed from Benares, the abominations of the temple are explained to intelligent natives as symbolical, dying pagans make continued faith in paganism on the part of their legatees a condition of their bequests. But all this indicates a fear that their religion is in danger.

And have we no success? Is it nothing that old pagan civilizations are crumbling; that religions originating centuries before the Christian are giving way at its advance; that people who boasted letters, and arts, and arms when our ancestors were painted savages, pursued in British woods or sold in Roman markets, are obedient to a Christian sovereign; that heathenism is every-where hedged about by civil law; that Juggernaut is deprived of his prey, and the widow saved from the funeral flames; that the sharks of the Ganges are suffering a famine of living human flesh; the priests often confessing that they minister only for their stomach's sake; the pundits declaring that there is nothing in the idol; that the whole population of the peninsula is accessible to Christian teaching; that pice will purge a man for contempt of caste; that missions are established in all the cities of the land, and school-houses planted in the hills and the valleys; that we have had an increase of forty-four thousand converts in the last disturbed decade; that sluggish mind is awaked from its sleep of ages; that Naamans, while they bow in the house of Rimmon, say in their hearts, "The Lord pardon thy servant in this thing;" that Mohammedan and Pagan Nicodemuses come to Christian teachers by night; that the pulpit, like the Master, is constrained to cry out, "Were there not ten cleansed, but where are the nine?"

Earth's birthday was when God said "Let there be light," though this light was diffused, penetrating the void, chasing the darkness, warming, preparing. It was not until the fourth day, after an earthly and heavenly convulsion, that God gathered the beams to their chambers in the sun, and showed the earth where her breast was warmed, the moon where her horns were filled with light, and day and night how their clocks were set. Soon may God collect the scattered beams, and make great lights in the moral firmament of India!

Suppose we had no success. Hath not God commanded, and shall not we obey? Has he promised immediate and invariable success? Christ divides the seed sown into four portions, only one of which brings forth abundant fruit. What if some of our seed fall by the wayside, or on the stones, or among thorns? Did the betrayal of Judas silence the apostles, or the denial of Peter ruin their cause? How many converts had Noah, though he preached righteousness by the century? And what shall we say of the prophets of whom the world was not worthy? And what of the Son of man, who closed his labors, crying, "O Jerusalem, how often would I have gathered thee as a hen gathereth her chickens under her wings, but ye would not!" and who, instead of blessing those only who succeed, said, "Blessed are they which are persecuted for righteousness?"

Suppose we had no reward, would we not preach? Can we see man debased, self-corrupted, self-mutilated, self-imbruted, self-damned, and not speak? Though no man hear and no man pity you must plead, though you tell your truth and sorrow to the stones. But this is not your case. India's sons are not strangers to thought nor to feeling. Beneath their caps they carry fertile brains, and under their ribs human hearts. Hypocritical, false, ungrateful from the oppression of ages they may be, but in their breasts is gentleness, and patience, and love, while religion enters largely into their national life. They have characteristics which if sanctified would enable them to enjoy the plerophory of grace. Europe is too proud, America too worldly, and both too materialistic. India, brought to Jesus, may lie like John in the Master's bosom. Is not the Indian mind, too, peculiarly adapted to our form of faith? It needs something to arouse it from its fatalism, to teach it the immutability of moral distinctions, the moral quality of intention, and to inspire it with a sense of human responsibility. It is adapted also to our type of piety, the emotional, the hopeful. It demands, too, our form of propagandism; we employ lay agency; we teach men to preach Christ crucified so soon as the divine coals burn within them. We have a system of itinerancy just fitted to set fire to these plains. If India is brought to God it must be chiefly through the agency of her own sons; and the sooner we take converted and called helpers to our confidence and commission them for our service the better. God forbid that we should hold them at arm's length! We have trusted such men in other hemispheres, we may in this. Train them, teach them, guide them, but send them forth. They will build churches over their heads, and map out self-sustaining circuits over these provinces.

The theism which is spreading here, and which inspires many good men with dread, but others more wise with encouragement, illustrates the national character. Unlike that of Europe, it pours itself out not in satire, and blasphemy, and spleen, but in prayers and pæans. It develops itself not in moral anarchy, but in church order.

We need not lower our standard for the sake of success. We sometimes envy Catholics their triumphs. It is their boast that Romanism took South America, and the aborigines became Christian, while Protestantism took North America, and the natives remain Pagan; that Romanism took Mexico, and it became religious; Protestantism took India, and it remains heathen or infidel. Moreover, that since Romanism entered India she has planted twenty vicariates and counted nearly a million converts. But what is the Christianity which she gives? We know many of her sons, and would be unjust to none. While she elevates man above Paganism and Mohammedanism, we must note that her monachism, holy water, baptismal regeneration, purgatory, pantheon, penance, priestly absolution, visible sacrifices, and gorgeous ceremonial, all tend to bring down Christianity to Paganism. My brethren, come not into her secret. When you report a convert let it be one in whom faith works by love to purify the heart. We can wait till by the fire of such walking evangels others shall light their lamps and set India ablaze.

Finally, brethren, be of one mind; live in peace; correspond with each other; bear with each other; love and help each other, and grapple to you the Church at home as with hooks, not merely of silver, but of love.

The controversies and divisions of the Church have greatly hindered the spread of truth. When every man has his psalm, his interpretation, his doctrine, the heathen is confused. One cried, "You must have as many Christs in America as there are gods in China." Let our peace and unity be manifest. We are happily situated. We occupy a field almost alone. We are within easy reach of each other, and we preach in a common language. Compare with ours the Presbyterian missions, stretched along a line of a thousand miles, among a people speaking at different points five different languages, while missions of other Churches intervene. The choice of the field and the organization of the missions reflect the highest credit on him whom the Church selected to lay her foundations in this land, and whom she will not fail to honor; and the prosperity of the missions indicates both the energy of the administration and the industry, and faithfulness, and ability of those who have worked the field.

And now Methodism is to organize her first Mission Conference on the soil of India; the continent on which Paradise bloomed, the ark rested, the law thundered, and the cross warmed with atoning blood; the land of prophets and apostles, of martyrs and mysteries, of the arts of man and the revelations of God. We bring back to her a Bible all whose pages were written on her soil, and are so illnstrated in her living customs that they may be read by the roadside without a commentator. We bring to her a religion whose first and fullest enjoyments were felt in the hearts of her noblest sons.

The location of our Conference is worthy of remark. We meet beneath earth's loftiest mountains. If the Lord's house were established in the top of the mountains, we should be under the droppings of its sanctuary. I stood upon the top of Cheena, and looked over a field of mountains, their bosoms encompassed by the fir, the pine, the cedar, and the sál, but their heads cold and bare granite, embraced by a semicircle of the snowy range whose peaks rise from twenty-three thousand to twenty-five thousand feet high, covered with eternal snow, on which the foot of man never trod, and never will tread. I walked a few paces and looked down upon the plain of the Ganges, stretching out like an immense ocean fringed with sea-weed, but with no sign of life. And yet I knew that in the mountains on the one side there beat six hundred thousand human hearts, and in the plains on the other fifty millions; and I said, "These all belong to Christ." The voice of the prophet came over me: "The idols shall he utterly abolish;" and the voice of the Father, "Ask of me and I shall give thee the heathen for thine inheritance, and the uttermost parts of the earth for thy possession;" and that other voice, "A nation shall be born in a day"—a prophecy to be realized in the crystallized civilizations of the East. We have had the planting, and it has been long; the harvest may come soon. There is a plant which it requires a century to mature, but it blossoms in a day. God has great and precious promises that have not yet been fulfilled. "He will arise to shake terribly the earth." Already I hear the precursors of the coming storm, and see the idols swept before the flood, and the whole land rising as by a divine force into light and love.

Now unto Him that is able to keep us from falling, and to present us faultless before his presence with exceeding joy, be all honor, might, majesty, and dominion, now, henceforth, and forever! Amen.

VII.

GENERAL REMARKS ON INDIA.

THAT immense triangle stretching from the Himalayas to Cape Comorin, a distance of nineteen hundred miles, and from the Hindoo Coosh on the west to the borders of Burmah on the east, a distance of fifteen hundred, is, in many respects, the grandest peninsula on earth. It has an area of 1,446,576 square miles, and is much larger than France, Great Britain, Austria, Germany, Portugal, Spain, Denmark, Greece, Switzerland, Holland, Belgium, Italy, Turkey, Prussia, and the Ionian Republic, united.

It is divided by the Vindhya Mountains into Hindostan and the Deccan, each of which has a table-land and plains. The table-land of the former is supported on the south by the Vindhya range, and on the north by a lower one in the Bundlecund, sloping gradually into the basin of the Ganges. The table-land of the Deccan, fifteen hundred feet above the sea level, is supported on the north by the Vindhya, and on the other three sides by the Ghats, which run round the peninsula near the coast, leaving low plains between their bases and the sea. The Nerbuddah River forms the dividing line between the two table-lands; the Warda marks the southern boundary of a woody tract which is peopled by aboriginal tribes; the Godavery flows through a valley that might supply the world with sugar; the Indus makes an Egypt in the north-west. Eastward of this stream, and westward of the Aravalli chain, lies a desert, with here and there an oasis.

Between the ranges of the Himalaya and the Vindhya mountains is the plain of the Ganges, with the Punjab at its head and Bengal at its foot, the latter of which seems to be the united gift of the Ganges and the Burrampootra. This great peninsula is walled in on the north by the snowy range of the Himalaya, and protected both on the east and west by mountain chains; and although it has gates alike on the east, the north-west, and the west, through which the Affghan the Tartar, and the Persian invasions have a different periods poured upon the plains below, yet with the instruments and science of modern warfare these passes may readily be guarded.

Off its southern extremity lies the fragrant

island of Ceylon, sustaining the same relation to India that Sicily does to Italy.

This fair land, extending from the eighth parallel of north latitude to the thirty-sixth, furnishes almost every vegetable, animal, and mineral product. Cereals abound in the plains, gems in the mountains, spices in the breeze; tea in Assam, coffee in the Nilgherry Hills, indigo in Bengal, and opium and jute in the basin of the Ganges. As to cotton and sugar, they are both indigenous to India, which, under improved methods of cultivation and of intercommunication, and a wise government, could stock the markets of the world with both commodities.

Although the *manufactures* of India, through want of proper encouragement, have declined, yet its muslins and works in the precious metals are still unrivaled, as well for their texture as their beauty.

The *population* of India is thus estimated:

British territory in India, ...	131,990,901
Native " "	48,376,247
French and Portuguese, ...	517,149
Total, ...	180,884,297

Dwell for a moment upon these figures. Suppose Providence take India from Great Britain, and, as a compensation, give her all the rest of

Asia, the Chinese empire alone excepted. Would she gain or lose as to the number of her subjects? Let us see. Arabia, with its celebrated deserts and mountains, and famed cities and unconquered tribes, contains eight millions. Asiatic Turkey, land of the Bible, the primitive seat of civilization, the scene of great victories and seat of great monarchies, ten millions; Georgia, two; Persia, nine; Affghanistan, six; Beeloochistan, one; Independent Tartary, seven; Siberia, stretching from sea to sea, three; Farther India, including Burmah, the kingdom of Siam, the empire of Anam, Cochin China, and Malacca, twenty millions; the Japan empire, thirty. Add these together and you have not much more than half the population of India. Set down now, in addition, Thibet, and Chinese Tartary, and Corea, and all other parts of the Chinese empire except China proper, say thirty-four millions, and you have one hundred and thirty millions. Next throw in Borneo, Sumatra, Java, the Philippine Isles, Celebes, Spice Islands, Floris, Timor—all Malaisia; next Australia, New Guinea, New Zealand, Van Dieman's Land, Louisiade, New Britain—all Australasia; then the Sandwich Islands, Society Islands, the Ladrone Islands—all Polynesia; in fine, Oceanica, one whole quarter of the globe, and you only raise the number to one hundred and fifty-six millions; still thirty-four millions short of the population of India.

Take another view. The Barbary States, Belud ul Gered, Egypt, Nubia, Abyssinia, Sahara, Soudan, Eastern Africa, Western Africa, Ethiopia, and the African Islands, all contain, according to our books generally, but sixty-two millions. To the population of Africa add that of Greenland, Iceland, British America, Russian America, Mexico, the United States, Central America, the West Indies, Bermudas, Brazil, Argentine Republic, New Grenada, Peru, Bolivia, Venezuela, Patagonia, Equador, Chili, Guiana, Uraguay, Paraguay, and the Falkland Islands, in fine, the whole continent of America, seventy millions in all, and you have only one hundred and thirty millions, more than fifty millions short of the population of India. Add to the people of both these continents those of Oceanica, and you raise the number to only one hundred and fifty-four millions, thirty millions less than India.

These people are of different origins, customs, and faiths, and speak various languages, not less than twenty-nine, twenty-four of them derived from the Sanscrit, and five from other sources. They have much knowledge and a wonderful history. India's astronomy dates fifteen centuries before Christ, and long ere the mind of the Mediterranean awoke. Her trigonometry was a thousand years in advance of that of Europe. Her logic and philosophy preceded and inspired those of Greece. The fascinating Pantheism which Germany elaborates, and England servilely echoes, and Emerson discourses as if it were a new discovery, has been proclaimed for two or three thousand years among a people to enlighten whose darkened minds Berlin, and London, and Boston send missionaries, and many a dirty devotee expounds it more adroitly, ay, and eloquently, too, than either.

The intellect of India is still the speculative mind of the East, sustaining the same relation to Asia that Greece does to ancient Europe, and Germany to modern. The Hindoos, a people of Caucasian origin, and of Indo-Germanic family, entering India through the Hindoo Coosh, three thousand years ago, and gradually spreading over the country, enslaving or driving to the southern mountains the aboriginal inhabitants, introduced Brahminism. This is a magnificent polytheism, systematic in form, with power to modify science, mold art, inspire literature, shape social life, sustain civil government, identify itself with nationality, and appeal to the strongest feelings of the native character, reverence for the past. Its hymns of devotion and formulas of worship, the

Vedas, four in number, are older than the Psalms of David, strongly imbued with patriarchal theology, deemed eternal, and supposed to have been written in the language of the gods. The Shasters, six in number, contain some scientific treatises, and a cosmogony in many respects reminding us of the book of Genesis, though it divides eternity, and gives us eras of millions of years. It has a theology resting upon the triad Brahma, Vishnu, and Shiva.

The language in which the sacred books are written—Sanscrit—is of unfathomable antiquity, and, according to Sir William Jones, more perfect than the Greek, more copious than the Latin, and more excellently refined than either; and, in the judgment of the learned, capable of expressing every movement of the human will, every form of human thought, and every wave of human passion, with unsurpassed clearness, elegance, and force.

The deities of Hindooism are generally worshiped in shapes in which they are supposed to have become incarnate. The popular theology is founded upon the code of Menu and the Puranas. The latter, eighteen in number, is a collection of legends concerning the gods, who marry, quarrel, sin, and suffer, and are thirty millions strong.

There is a striking resemblance between the earlier mythology of India and that of ancient Egypt, Greece, and Rome. Thus Brahma corresponds to the Ammon of the Egyptians, the Zeus of the Greeks, the Jupiter of the Romans; Saraswati to the Neith of Egypt, the Athena of Greece, the Minerva of Rome; Cama to Cupid; Chrishna with the Gopias dancing around him, to Apollo and the Muses; Rama to the Osiris of Egypt and the Bacchus of Greece. Shiva in India becomes Typho in Egypt, and Pluto in Greece; while the Isa of the first land is the Isis of the second, and the Diana of the third. Transmigration is modified in the west into Tartarus and the shades of Elysium, and absorption into the Deity into ascent to the gods. Both the East and the West believed that man had a prior existence, and they taught the doctrine of purification by punishment; but the Greeks, too busy with this world, postponed purgatory to the next; while the Hindoos preferred torture on this side the grave to Pluto and his fires on the other. The gods and myths of India were probably the originals of which those of the classic West were the copies. The latter are now known only to song, the former still live in the faith of the people. The types of Osiris and Bacchus, of Isis and Diana, are still worshiped under the shade of mango groves, and the descendant of the original bull Apis may be seen in every Hindoo city, and under the shadow of every temple of Shiva. Whether Indian mythology is older or not, it is supe rior to the European. While the Grecian gods become incarnate for purposes of lust, prejudice, or passion, those of India come in flesh for purposes of benevolence. Is Vishnu a fish? It is to rescue truth from a demon, or humanity from the deluge. Is he a tortoise? It is to sustain the earth when sinking in the ocean. Is he a boar? It is to draw forth upon his tusks the land that had been submerged. Is he a lion bursting from the marble column? It is to save a pious son from the hands of a blaspheming monarch. Is he a dwarf? It is to serve the gods. Is he a warrior? It is to destroy oppressors. Does he become Ram? It is to overcome Ravanna and liberate Ceylon. Does he appear as Krishnu? It is to slay monsters and demons, and abound in benefactions. Is he a Buddha? It is to counteract perverted power. In his future incarnation—Kalki—he is to come on a white horse to restore pure religion, punish the impenitent, and bring back the golden age.

The substance of these mythologies is the same, whether modified by the gloomy mind of

India, the heavy one of Egypt, the cheerful one of Greece, or the stately and steady one of Rome; and this substance is evidently of higher antiquity than any—a primitive revelation. The existence of God, the garden of Eden, the fall of man, a future state, an incarnation, a possibility of reunion with God, the certainty of punishment, and the doctrine of substitution, may be traced through them all, but perverted and obscured. The Supreme Being is often exhibited without attributes, the void. Depravity is from the evil nature of matter; the future state is substituted by transmigration; and pardon and purification are sought by ceremonies, contemplation, self-torture, and presents to priests. The ancient mythologies are the solid gold of truth beaten into flimsy tinsel, and molded by a depraved imagination into forms which dazzle and bewilder, but are no longer capable of being the current coin of the moral universe, or bearing the image of its Maker.

This history of Indian idolatry, and indeed of all, shows that when men forsake revelation their minds grow darker and darker. There is an awful descent from the Vedas to the Institutes of Menu, and a still greater from these to the Puranas.

The greater permanence of Indian religion is

due, in great measure, to the fact that while the spiritual ideas of Greece and Rome assumed the fascinating but perishable forms of statuary and painting, those of India took the enduring form of books. The original volumes, however, being in a language unknown to the common people, are, so far as they are concerned, dead.

The living and degenerated faith has defiled the whole literature of the land. I once asked why native ladies were not educated. The answer was, "There is no literature in the language fit for a lady to read." The common thoughts and conversation of the people are defiled.

Nor is this surprising when we consider their god and myths, or even their temples. It is creditable to the modesty of Indian women that they visit the temples at night. How they pass the streets without blushing it is difficult to tell, for the public places are made odious by the objects of adoration set up within them. Behold the steps of descent. Beginning with the true God, they advanced to the triad, then multiplied their avatars, finally worshiped things inanimate, till now the waters, the sun, the monkey, are worshiped, and the gods of the country are more numerous than the men, while the objects most adored are those that are most disgusting. Their general conduct is what we might expect, according to the spirit that now worketh in the children of disobedience. They have indeed a standard of morality, falling below which one is condemned, for "when the Gentiles do by nature the things contained in the law, these, having not the law, are a law unto themselves." Indeed, without this no business could be carried on, and no community exist. Hence, when the dhooley bearer receives his charge he takes the same care of it that a Christian would. But beyond the outward act it is to be feared the morality of Hindoos rarely goes. Little do they feel of love to God or to man, or the spirit of peace and good-will which the angels expressed at the birth of Jesus.

The institutions of Hindooism illustrate its character. Prominent among these is caste. The code of Menu divides society into four castes—the priest, the soldier, the husbandman, and the servant. The first was said to proceed from the mouth of Brahma, the second from his arms, the third from his thighs, and the fourth from his feet. These have almost disappeared except the first. The Brahmins, from ten to twelve millions, still, by monopoly of knowledge, maintain their position at the head of the social edifice, beneath which there are now numerous castes, varying from sixty to a hundred and seventy, according to locality.

How a system so utterly at war with fundamental, political, and Gospel principles could prevail for two thousand five hundred years is amazing, unless you consider that it is rooted in the popular religion, is deemed the divine order, and confers immunities on the lower castes in proportion to their descent in the social scale. The Brahmin is in perpetual danger of losing caste, for if he but touch a mehter's button he is defiled. The tenacity with which caste is held is wonderful. A Fakir, on being imprisoned, determined to starve himself to death, and die with a curse upon the magistrate upon his lips. When he was nearly gone, the jailer read to him an order that he should, when a corpse, be wrapped in an ox-hide, carried out by men of low caste, and buried in the earth; he immediately said, "Give me food, or I lose my caste." At Jyepore, in Rajpootana, a bazaar that could not be cleared with police or artillery was at once cleared by some sweepers with brooms. Sir John Lawrence, who attributes the Sepoy rebellion to the greased cartridges, related to me this story: On a field of battle an officer and a Sepoy lay side by side, wounded and suffering, in the hot sun. All day the Indian said nothing but "Water! water!" Toward night a woman came with a skin of water. The Englishman drank and was refreshed. The Sepoy asked the woman of what caste she was, and being informed that she was of low caste, he turned away his parched lips. The officer remonstrated, "You and I only are present; I pledge my honor as a soldier never to mention it. Drink, and you may live; refuse, and you die." "No," said he, "better die than lose my caste." If the Sepoy were a Brahmin, we may cease to wonder when we reflect that, according to the code of Menu, whatever exists in the universe is all in effect, though not in form, the wealth of the Brahmin, since he is entitled to it by his primogeniture and eminence in rank. To him knowledge is shut up, for the sacred books are too holy to be studied by any but a Brahmin, or even to be read by a Soodra. He who mentions a Brahmin with contumely should have an iron style, ten fingers long, thrust red-hot into his mouth.

Some, perhaps, may tell us that something exactly like this exists in this country, and that if we substitute a certain word for Brahmin, and a certain other for Soodra, we shall find here an unwritten code of the same spirit as that of Menu. I am aware that customs and feelings akin to caste may be found in the Christian world—as when a man is compelled to follow the trade of his father, or a people are doomed to inferiority in consequence of their color. But mark the difference: these things are *in defiance of Christianity.*

Kindred to caste is slavery, which has existed from time immemorial in India, and which, despite British law, exists there to this day, and to such an extent that there is scarcely a Rajah or wealthy native family that has not its slaves. Mark, this in accordance with the native religion; but where it exists in Christian lands it is contrary to conscience and faith, and destined, with the cultivation of the one and the progress of the other, to utter extermination. Suttee, the burning of the woman upon the funeral pile, was often done against her own remonstrance, and by means of her own children binding her to the flames. Infanticide is still practiced secretly by the Rajpoots and Kshatryas, in order to avoid the expense of marrying their daughters, and it is authorized by the sacrifices to the river god Gunga.

More terrible still is the practice of Thuggee—a system of hereditary murder, carried on by a fraternity spread all over India, having secret signs and a peculiar dialect, who are taught from boyhood to look upon murder by the noose as their calling. We have bands of robbers, counterfeiters, murderers, in Christian lands; but note the difference. The Thug is religiously inducted by his spiritual guide; he uses an instrument consecrated by religious solemnities. He worships Kali, a murderous goddess, who has given him the privilege of killing his fellow-beings for a livelihood, to whom after every murder he makes an offering of silver and of sugar, whose wrath he would incur if he failed, when the omens were favorable, to suffocate the victim, and whose name is so venerable with the people that the native rulers are afraid to deal with her murderers. Similar to this is the system of Dekoitee, practiced religiously by a set of robber castes.

These are *legitimate* moral results of Brahminism. I need not speak of polygamy, nor of the degradation of woman, nor of the monasticism and devoteeism so prevalent. The priests are often celibates and mendicants. The fakirs are numerous; some holding their hands clinched until the nails pass through the skin, others suspending themselves by hooks, others rolling themselves across the country, measuring hundreds of miles with their bodies.

The priests profess to worship not the idol

but God in the idol, as they pay homage to the queen in the person of the viceroy. They, however, seem to have no knowledge of the Infinite Being, who, they say, is incomprehensible to finite minds, and to whom, in all India, there is neither priest nor temple. The philosophers are generally pantheists, and teach either that both matter and spirit are manifestations of Brahma, or that Brahma is the only existence, and creation an illusion, or that matter is eternal, and Brahma, uniting himself with it, gives it life. Each system confounds God and the creature, and destroys all moral distinctions. The Vedants, when asked who is God, will generally point to themselves. They allege that if men lie or murder, it is not they, but God in them, that is chargeable. The common people do not reason much, but bow credulously before the idol.

India gave birth to another idolatrous system, Buddhism, which originated with Sakya Muni six hundred years before Christ. It is full of absurdities and false philosophy. It teaches the doctrine of transmigration, embraces no idea of forgiveness, asserts that punishment follows transgression as the cart-wheel follows the ox, enjoins the building of monasteries and temples, and the making and worshiping of gods, which deeds will elevate us to pleasant spheres where we may eat fruits and gather flowers reared by the hands of angels. It is, however, atheistic, and teaches that all things end in annihilation. Rejecting caste, it provoked the opposition of Brahminism, and after a long and fearful conflict it was driven out of India. It took refuge, however, in the island of Ceylon, the slopes of the Himalayas, and the table-land beyond, gradually spread along the eastern shores of the Bay of Bengal, and finally took root in China and Japan. It is now the faith of three hundred millions of the human race. It is seen in India now in a modified form called Jainism, which embraces caste. The number of Buddhists under the British government must be many millions, as the people of British Burmah, Ceylon, and Tennasserim are chiefly of that faith.

There is another great heresy, Mohammedism, that has also a strong hold in India. The false prophet had scarcely been in his grave fifty years before the Arabian cavalry was reined up on the banks of the Chenaub. Mahmoud of Ghuznee conquered Guzerat and the Punjab; Arabs and Abyssinians formed settlements upon the coast; Tamerlane sacked Delhi, and his descendants founded the Mohammedan dynasty of the great Mogul. Persian and Affghan invasions of Mussulmans from the West, and of Tartars from the

North, have also been seen, and rarely rolled back, from the Indian plains.

Of Mohammedism we need say but little. The Koran borrows facts and principles from the Bible, but incorporates with them fables and errors. It admits the truth that there is one God, but perverts it by representing him as equally the author of sin and holiness; it teaches a gloomy fatalism, and puts the Hadees or traditions before the Koran. Its moral code is cruel and bloody, and allows both slavery and polygamy; its worship consists of external ceremonies; it is without any plan of propitiation or pardon, and it holds out to the believer a paradise of carnal delights. The results of the system are terrible. I expected to find the Mohammedans more upright than the Pagans, inasmuch as their creed is better; but I was assured by credible testimony that they are more profligate, licentious, and cruel than their heathen neighbors, and they have introduced forms of sin into India too shameless to be named.

The Mussulman population of India is probably twenty-seven millions; among these, all the sects of that faith, Shiites, Sunnites, and Wahabees. In the shadow of these colossal forms of error you find various offshoots, such as the Sikh faith, and among the aboriginal inhabitants, idolaters who have not yet abandoned human sacrifices.

When mankind were dispersed the most populous and enterprising tribes moved eastward; thither was the path of empire. On the Euphrates, or beyond, arose the Assyrian, Babylonian, and other great kingdoms, and even before they arose the children of Noah had probably founded on the banks of the Hoang Ho the great empire of China. Arts and arms seemed to be the inheritance of Shem and Ham, and to find their first theaters in Asia or Africa. After a time the tents of Japheth began to grow powerful, and the scepter of the world to be transferred to the basin of the Mediterranean.

When our Lord ascended and gave gifts to men, he taught his disciples that his empire was universal, and, sending them forth into all the world, he exhibited to them in millennial vision the North, the South, the East, and the West sitting down together in the kingdom of God. They obeyed his command. While some went north, others south, and others west, a few penetrated the denser and darker populations of the East. But upon the sun-worshipers of Persia, and the philosophic Pagans of India and China, they seem to have made little or no impression. Turn to the map of the countries traveled by the apostles, as the historian has traced it, and you will observe that it does not extend eastward of the Orontes. Westward from Calvary has been the march of Christianity, through Asia Minor, around the Ægean, over the classic soil of Greece and Macedonia, and the peninsula of Italy, and still westward through Spain, Gaul, Scandinavia, Great Britain, and still westward over North and South America.

Account for it as we may, the East has stubbornly rejected the Word of Life. Neither the idolatrous systems of classic Rome and Greece, which had no Bible, nor the rude superstitions of Gaul and Goth, and Celt and Briton, whose divinities were local, nor the fetichism of Africa, nor the spirit-worship of aboriginal America, has presented such formidable obstacles to the religion of Christ as are found in the lands of the East.

There stand Brahminism, Buddhism, Mohammedism—systems in which philosophy and superstition, priestcraft and kingcraft, have combined their powers to rule the human mind, and which stand like moral Himalayas against the march of truth.

Although in the days of John the Revelator the eastern nations contained the bulk of mankind, as they have done ever since, yet they are not once named in the Apocalypse.

The reason is apparent. The Bible gives no account of nations but as they are connected with the Church; and God, foreseeing that the peoples of the East would resist the truth until they were finally put into the power and under the tutelage of Christian rulers, saw also that their history, so far as connected with the history of redemption, would be a part of that of the Western powers. God governs nations as we govern men. He uses moral means first, then physical. He will give to his Church the heritage of the heathen, if not by mercy, then by power. When he set up his king upon his holy hill of Zion, he declared the decree, and threatened to break those nations to pieces that disregarded it. When the Jews crucified Messiah, destruction fell alike upon their city, temple, and nation. So Roman emperors went down one after another, until a Christian ascended the imperial throne. God bore long with the lands of the East, but he has at length taken them in hand.

Russian guns upon the banks of the Amoor, English and French at the gates of Pekin, have broken down the walls which so long barred China from the rest of the world. The thunders of artillery have also opened the way through the empire of Japan, not only for commerce, but for science and religion. By being brought within the range of cannon, Australia and the islands of the sea have been brought within the range of truth. But the most remarkable instance in which God has broken nations like a potter's vessel is India—that land in which, as a focal point, the three colossal systems of religious error converge and radiate.

Nothing in history is more wonderful than that a clerk in a factory should win one of the largest empires in the world; that a trading corporation should for so many years hold and acquire territory as did the East India Company; that, having failed to accomplish its purposes, it was overthrown by one of the bloodiest revolutions the world has ever seen; that such a revolution should be put down by a little island nine thousand miles distant; that it should prove to be the grandest step in India's progress; and that one hundred and eighty millions of Pagans should be easily and safely governed by eighty thousand Christian sabers. This is the Lord's doings, and it is marvelous in our eyes; none the less so because wicked men have accomplished the work, often from bad motives, and by unjustifiable means. God knows how to use bad men, and overrule bad motives and deplorable events for the welfare of the world. Among angels, progress doubtless is through reason, and by the path of peace; but, owing to the perversity of man, national preservation and progress are by violence. What prevented Asiatic despotism from overspreading Europe? What prevented ancient Rome from becoming Punic? What saved mediæval Germany and Gaul from becoming Mohammedan? What prevented the United States from being the great slave empire, and the propagandist of despotism in its worst form? Arms. The elements of our civilization—Greek culture, Roman law, Christian morals, Protestant faith, and political freedom—were all both procured and preserved by steel. What wonder, then, if God break down with a rod of iron those despotisms which for three thousand years have doomed the East to superstition, sluggishness, idolatry, and corruption, and prepare the peoples for a baptism of water by a baptism of blood?

Will the ascendency of the British in India be permanent? Yes. How came they to put down the rebellion? The people were divided. The masses, long oppressed, cared nothing for the issue. Had they simply retired from their villages to the interior, carrying their effects with them, the British army must have starved to death by the roadside. But it was well supplied.

Besides this division between the ruler and the ruled, there were others. The Bengali hates the Madrasse, both despise the natives of Bombay, all three look with jealousy upon the hardier race of the North-West Provinces, while the Sikhs and Ghoorkas have little respect for any of the rest, or they for them. Then there are religious divisions. Mohammedans and Brahmins can never unite. Though they joined the mutiny with the watchword, "Two faiths in one saddle," the Brahmin soon perceived that the back seat was for him. The Mohammedans themselves are divided into Sunnites, Shiites, and Wahabees; and the Hindoos into nearly two hundred castes and eighty-four thousand sects, whose interests are diverse. The intelligent Rajahs perceive the advantages of English rule, and shudder at the anarchy and conflicts that would ensue from its overthrow. Meanwhile, while the natives are disarmed, the British have a controlling army and full possession of all the strongholds of the country, and are strengthened by perhaps twenty-five thousand European residents and a hundred thousand Eurasians.

What will this power effect? Judge by what it has already effected. It has reduced anarchy to order, given law, established justice, protected the land from invasion, and prevented it from being ravaged by intestine wars. It has suppressed Suttee and Dekoitee, forbidden human sacrifices, repressed infanticide, and made slavery illegal. It has woven a network of telegraphs around the empire from Galle to Peshawur, and from Peshawur to Rangoon. It has established a regular system of postage for letters, papers, and books at low charges and uniform rates. It has improved old roads, and made new ones; sent steamers up the principal streams; constructed a canal nine hundred miles long, and will probably soon construct others in the valleys of the Mahanuddy, the Kistna, and the Godavery. It has commenced a system of railways embracing about five thousand miles of trunk lines, at a cost of nearly three thousand millions of dollars, which, when completed, will unite the extremes of the peninsula, open hitherto inaccessible tracts, and bring all parts close to each other and to the civilized world. Already the steam-horse traverses the peninsula from Calcutta to Bombay, crosses the peninsula from Madras to the western shore, and prances from Bombay to Nagpore.

It has steadily increased the trade of the country, which, before the days of Clive, could be conveyed in a single Venetian frigate, until it now reaches nearly five hundred millions of dollars annually. It has raised the revenues of the Government to two hundred and fifteen millions. It has given India the newspaper—that great educator—so that there are twenty-eight newspapers published weekly in Bengal—three of them in English, by the natives—thirty native presses in Madras, and I know not how many in Bombay and Ceylon, and twenty-five presses among the missions alone. It has established schools in all parts of the land, in which those sciences are taught that undermine the prevailing systems of superstition and error. It has made the English language classical in the country, and by this means it is furnishing the native mind with the rich and Christian stores of which that noble tongue is the medium. It has protected missionaries of Christ and their converts.

Since the mutiny eight or ten new missionary societies have entered India, bringing large additions to its evangelizing forces, so that in 1862, according to Dr. Mullins, there were in British India, including Burmah and Ceylon, 31 societies, working in 386 stations and 2,307 out-stations; 541 missionaries; 186 native missionaries; 1,776 catechists; 1,542 native churches; 49,688 communicants; 213,182 native Christians;

48,390 vernacular day-schools; 23,963 boys in Anglo-vernacular schools; 39,647 girls in day and boarding schools, showing an increase of over forty thousand Christians in ten years. Meanwhile the Bible has been translated into fourteen different languages of India, and circulated to the extent of 1,634,940 copies, and other Christian publications to that of 10,000,000.

Look, then, at this great peninsula, linked to the continent and the world by its languages, commerce, and religions; source of false faiths which together insnare six hundred millions of the human race, and the stronghold of a delusion that blinds a hundred and eighty millions more. This great moral pest-house, this Babel of devils, God has put into the power of one of the most enlightened Christian nations on earth. There are more Mohammedans under Victoria's scepter than under any other on earth. The Sultan has but twenty-one millions; she has twenty-five millions at least. There are more heathen under the same Christian queen than under any sovereign, except the emperor of China. And this mass is all through and through, and more and more, subjected to Christian influences. The telegraphs are so many ganglia in a great nervous system, diffusing new sensations; the railways are so many iron arteries, pumping Christian blood through the native veins; the newspapers are so many digestive powers, preparing healthful moral food; the schools are so many batteries, thundering at the crumbling battlements of error; the missions are so many brains, thinking new and better thoughts.*

Knowledge must be diffused through the earth. We know two things more; namely, that our religion can withstand modern science and make it tributary to itself, and that no other religion can; for every other faith has linked its science with its doctrines, so that they must both fall together. As to take Paris is to take France, and to take Sebastopol is to shake Russia to the Arctic seas, and to take Richmond is to shake out the rebels of the United States from the Potomac to the Rio Grande, so to Christianize India, owing to its key position in heathendom, is to shake out the idols from the face of the whole earth.— Intellectual and moral power has both rights and responsibilities, and it is destined to rule the earth under the providence of God. Should Christian nations do for China what England has done for India, would not the people be wiser, better, happier? would not the boundaries of science, philosophy, and true religion be

* The annual expenditure for missions is $1,400,000, and the expenditure of the Government for schools about the same.

enlarged, and all the best interests of the world be promoted? Should the decrepit empire of the Sultan perish, and Great Britain receive Egypt and the Barbary States, France Asia Minor, and Russia European Turkey, who does not see that peoples long oppressed and darkened would be delivered, enlightened, raised to a higher and nobler civilization, brought into more intimate communion with mankind, and made to contribute immensely more to the wealth, the wisdom, and the worth of the world? They may do wrongs which may justify superior nations in exercising power over them; and if they give to them governments better adapted to their condition, and fitted to secure the protection of all their interests, let us bid them Godspeed.

We have entered upon a grand era. The Almighty is shaking the nations preparatory to giving them to his Son. The lines both of prophecy and providence converge at a point to which our feet are rapidly tending. In the new dispensation to which we hasten India will be a grand actor.

VIII.

OUR FIELD IN INDIA.

FROM the general survey of India, let us take a particular survey of our particular field.

Our mission field in Hindostan lies between the 25th and 30th parallels of North latitude. It is chiefly in the plain of the Ganges, though it crosses the Terai, and embraces a part of the lower spurs of the great chain of mountains on the north. Westward and southward it is bounded by the Sacred River, which, issuing from a chasm in the Himalayas at Hurdwar, proceeds, first southward, then south-eastward, to the Delta. Through this district, in a south-eastern course, flow the Goomtee, the Gogra, the Saee, the Ramgunga, and the Raptee. Our field extends from east to west, 400 miles, and from north to south, nearly 150 miles.

With the exception of the jungle and a portion of the hills beyond, it is all arable, and is the richest soil in India; consisting mainly of a rich alluvial mold, and containing gold in some localities, and saltpeter and lime in others. The climate during the months of November and December, when I was there, was delightful. The sun rose day after day without a cloud, marched up to the zenith and down to the horizon undimmed, and set with promise of a brilliant dawn. Nowhere did I ever see Aurora unbar the gates of the East on goodlier hinges, or spread beauty over the landscape with more gentleness and serenity. Indeed, the blue sky, the green earth, the gay gardens, the many-colored fields ripening to the harvest, the mango groves alive with playful monkeys, the orchards displaying their variegated fruits beneath dark-green foliage festooned with the plumage of Oriental birds, and the still warm air, sweet with a thousand perfumes, reminded me of Paradise itself. True, this is the best season of the year. There are periods—July to November—when warm rains almost incessantly fall; and others—March to June—when dusty and sultry winds blow from the west, or damp ones, laden with the malaria of Bengal or Assam, from the east, and when constitutions accustomed to more temperate latitudes languish; but with proper precautions and appropriate comforts, even these seasons may be safely passed. The thermometer rarely rises above 112 degrees Fahrenheit. Many Europeans in health and vigor are found here, and many Caucasians, well developed and active, both in body and mind, claim this fair region as their native land. The children of the English are usually sent home to be educated, but it is that they may escape the corrupting influences of the social and religious life of the East rather than the enervating effect of its climate. At Benares, our hostess, though born in India, is healthy, remarkably fair, and blessed with offspring as promising as herself. At Lukempore we met a native of English parentage who would compare favorably with European ladies in all respects. At Allahabad, our hostess, of English stock and Indian birth, has thirteen vigorous children, and is so healthy, beautiful, and vivacious, that one might suppose she may be the mother of thirteen more. We met with many soldiers in India who were in good health, and though anxious to return to England, this was rather because they were weary of military life than tired of the country.

It is well to note that the mission field is not exclusively in the plain of the Ganges, but embraces some hill territory. This affords an opportunity for those missionaries who have been exhausted by the climate of the lowlands to renovate themselves without surceasing from their labors. Our field contains two choice spots for Sanitaria; namely, Nynee Tal and Pouri. The former is built around a lake six thousand feet above the level of the sea, in a mountain basin on which magnificent peaks cast their shadows. Looking up when the morning is moist, you may see their summits putting on their misty hoods as a judge puts on his powdered wig, or ascending an eminence you may look down and see the clouds below you encompassing the mountain bosom like a girdle. Around the picturesque lake of pure water, with fish in its caves and fowl on its surface, runs a graveled road, on part of which is a bazaar.

From the shore up the mountain sides, wherever the situation is favorable for building, rise palatial residences in European style, though modified to adapt them to a warm climate. Thither English officers and their families resort in the hot season, and find a bracing air, a charming scenery, and facilities for swimming, racing, boating, hunting, fishing, cricket, and other athletic amusements. Ladies may ride around the lake on fleet horses, or, taking a jampan, visit the mountain gorges, or by an ascent of five miles reach the top of Cheena, and after looking down two thousand feet to the lake, or eight thousand to the plains, may, by walking a short distance over a grassy platform, look up twenty-one thousand to the snowy range of the Himalayas, stretching half round the horizon in a vast amphitheater, rising to the heavens as if to support the throne of the Almighty, and inclosing within their semicircle a field of mountains of lower elevation, up whose sides climb the yew, the holly, the pine, and the cedar, here and there creeping up the crevices nearly to the cold granite tops.

Should the company linger till evening, they will pause in their descent to mark the shadows cast by the mountains upon one another, and the pink tints of such slopes as are exposed to the setting sun, and to ride in those chariots of God, the clouds, as they rise from the valleys, but not to reach the peaks covered with eternal snow. Earth has no spot better fitted to invigorate both body and mind. Here we should build a spacious house for our missionaries, that thither, while weary pilgrims of the plain, they may cast their longing eyes, and there may tune their divine harps when they are unstrung.

Our field is as fruitful as it is fair. It produces wheat, maize, barley, grain, various species of dahl, bajra, peas, beans, mustard seed, from which oil is made, the castor-oil bean, til, rice, cotton, indigo, and opium. Several vegetables have been introduced from Europe, such as the tomato and potato. The fruits are numerous, healthful, and luscious, among which are the mango, the guava, the banana, the plantain, the tac, the lime, the pumalo, the tamarind, the custard apple, the pine-apple, the apricot, the plum, the pear, the peach, the orange, the musk-melon, the water-melon, the pomegranate. Small fruits, such as grapes, raspberries, and strawberries, abound. In the lowlands we find the bamboo, and in the forests the sissoo, toon, beech, sycamore, chestnut, acacia, oak, pepul, nim, saul, and various species of palm, while here and there we see the sandal shed its odors, and the banyan spread its ample arms and arches.

The shrubs are numerous, and many, such as the box, the mandy, the cactus, and the jait, are used for hedges. The flowers most common are the balsam, the convolvulus, the heart's-ease, the mimosa, the fuchsia, the amaranth, the wax-flower, and the aloe. Roses are found all the year, and marigolds are extensively cultivated, as they are used in the temples, both to adorn the worshipers and to be cast upon the shrines. Animal life abounds. Of the horse, you may meet with the tatoo, the mule, the Cabul steed, a fine creature; the Australian, a large one; the

Arabian, a fleet one, though the climate will not allow any of them to be used, except very moderately. The animals chiefly employed for draft are the ox, of Tartary, and the buffalo. The elephant is used by those who can afford it. Near the cities may be seen donkeys, in long lines, with panniers upon their backs; camels in droves, laden with the traffic of the West, and tied by ropes extending from the tail of one to the nose of the next. Now and then a swift camel may be seen with a skillful rider upon his back, carrying express messages from camp to camp, at the rate of ten miles an hour and a hundred a day. Sheep follow their shepherds to the plain, and goats of great variety range the mountains; swine, lean and lank, are driven from gutter to gutter by swineherds, now, as in the Savior's time, deemed the lowest of mankind; the shepherd dog is with the flock, and the mastiff at the door; the mongoose seizes the snake, as he moves through the grass; jackals, foxes, porcupines, and hares start from the thicket; the wild elephant and boar, roused by the passing dhooley, and alarmed by the sight of the musalch and the shout of the coolies, rush into the jungle; the wolf often enters the village and carries off an aged person or stray child; the leopard leaps upon his unsuspecting victim; the tiger watches by rock or stream for the passing pilgrim; the bear, black, brown, or white, according to elevation, ranges the mountains; eagles perch upon the peaks, vultures fight over the carcasses of city or field; cranes, storks, swans, ducks, and kingfishers are seen by the streams; parrots and peacocks adorn the groves; quails and partridges run through the heather; cocks crow before the door; geese cackle at the barn; and crows hover over the fields or alight upon the half-burned bodies floating down the rivers. Fishes swarm the streams, and crocodiles and sharks watch at their mouths; worms spin their silk, or distill their lac; musquitoes sting the unwary traveler; locusts devastate large tracts of country; while white ants honeycomb the cutcha walls, tunnel beams and rafters, consume carpets and books, literally destroying houses and consuming their furniture. A banker, who had a large deficit, charged it to profit and loss account, saying that the ants had eaten up his missing bags of silver, though the stockholders were rather incredulous on the subject. It is astonishing that such little creatures can do such mischief. They are small, soft, gelatinous, and the birds devour them by the thousand, as if they were masses of jelly, and yet there is scarcely a beam—unless it be of sal timber—or a wall through which they will not make their passage. They often push their march through solid columns of burnt brick.

But it is time to speak of the noblest animal. The population of our field is set down at fifteen millions. Politically they belong to the late kingdom of Oude, the province of Rohilcund, the native state of Rampore, and the hill provinces of Ghurwall and Kumaon. They are of black color, graceful forms, straight hair, and Caucasian features. Physically, they are handsomer than the tribes of the Deccan, and stronger than the Bengalese or the Madrassese; morally, they are braver, prouder, more warlike than all, consisting largely of the Rohillas and Rajpoots, tribes noted for their daring and prowess, and having among them a considerable number of Mohammedans, a people every-where distinguished both for energy and arrogance. Both Rohillas and Mussulmans entered the country sword in hand, and though subdued, have not been conquered. The long conflict between the Talookdars and the cultivators of this region trained both to arms, and made most of them professional robbers.

From this quarter, chiefly, the British obtained the Sepoys with which they filled up the lines of the Bengal army. There are over a million of people in the district of Roy Bareilly, and only one large town in it. This fact is attributed to the circumstance that under Mohammedan rule this part of the country was inhabited by a tribe from which the king's troopers were taken. It was comparatively lawless, and it rendered both life and property insecure, so that a few years ago it was dangerous to go even through the city unarmed.

The people of the hills are industrious, provident, and happy. Every man seems to have his wife, and cow, and little plot of land, generally three acres. In the cold season they go down to the plains with their flocks, furniture, and families, and engage in some useful labor till the return of Spring. The women are often seen at the roadside bearing burdens upon their heads. I have seen them carrying stone from the quarries in this way.

The civilization of our whole field is quite different from American. The houses are usually mud or unburnt brick, the walls rising six or seven feet above the roof to form an inclosed court for the women, which is protected during the rains by a temporary covering of bamboo. The floors are of earth, and the rooms are without ceiling. We often find a court in the rear of the habitation, where the goats and cattle find refuge at night, the cooks prepare the meals, and the family sleep during the hot season, safe from wolves, who avoid walls, fearing traps inside.

Some of the farms have low walls, or fences made of mud, or hedges, but usually they have no inclosures. A sort of crate on four high poles overlooks each plantation, and here sits a watchman with a long whip to frighten off intruders, whether biped or quadruped, usually the former, as the flocks and herds are attended by their keepers. The agricultural implements, plow, harrow, roller, wooden spade, axes, two inches by four, sharp-pointed hoe, small sickle, and grass-cutter, are usually of the rudest kind. The plow merely scratches the ground, and the harrow is often only the branch of a tree, though the earth is frequently prepared for the seed with a spade. Fertilizers and rotation of crops are rarely employed. Stock is kept to a limited extent only, as the religious prejudices of the people prevent the use of animal food. The ordure of field and stable, strange to say, is used either for fuel or sacred purposes. The lower classes will eat mutton and fowl when they can obtain it. The British are slowly introducing improvements; the labor of man is, however, too cheap to afford much encouragement to the introduction of machinery. Our missionaries once introduced an American plow, but the cattle could not draw it. No pumps or windlasses are used in the wells, the water is drawn either by human hand or by cattle. Women still sit at the mill, and the sound of the grinding is heard every morning. The grain is trodden out by oxen, and winnowed in large baskets, or in blankets shaken by men. Burdens are generally borne upon the head. In crossing the Jumna I saw hundreds—men, women, and children—carrying earth upon their heads, in little baskets, to lay the foundations of the abutments. If you were to give them wheelbarrows they would probably use them in the same way. Freight is conveyed either in this manner or on bamboos. The bridges are pontoon, and the boats often wear canvas hewed out of seisam logs. By the institution of caste, laborers are so classified that every gentleman's house needs a dozen servants or more. The bearer takes care of the house furniture and lamps; the kitmutgar buys and prepares the food; the musalche is a subordinate to the kitmutgar in the kitchen; the mehter sweeps the floors and attends to the bath-rooms; the syce cares for the horse and drives it; the grass-cutter provides for the stable, since no hay is made in India; the beestee draws and carries the water; the dhoby washes the clothes;

the durzee—tailor—makes and mends the garments; the chokedar watches through the night the house and aviary; the ayah has charge of the nursery; the mettrannie is the chambermaid; and the two punkah-wallahs pull the fans which are needed in the hot season. The above are all that are found in missionary families, and of these the durzee and the punkah-wallah are not needed more than half the time. Should any think this force too great, let him try it. But, in addition to these, rich European families have a khansana or steward, a chuprasse or messenger, a dhai or wet nurse, and an extra bearer, ayah, cook, durzee, and from two to ten syces, according to the number of horses kept, making a staff of from twenty-three to thirty servants, besides the coolies necessary to bear the jampan or the dhooley, when one goes where the roads do not admit of carriages. This staff is not, as we might suppose, ruinous. The wages are, per month, taking the servants in the above order, $2.50, $4, $3, $2, $2.50, $2, $2, $3.50, $2, $2, $4, $2, $1.50, amounting to $33; but as punkah-wallahs are not constantly needed, and as the syce is often grass-cutter also, say $28. As these laborers support themselves, you perceive that their united cost is not equal to that of one hired girl among us.

Manufactures in India are by slow and coarse processes, but the patience and skill of the artisans make up for the imperfection of their instruments. In cotton and silk, fine fabrics are found in northern cities; in gold and silver works, the shops of Delhi are unrivaled; in furniture, Bareilly is scarcely surpassed; at Secrora you meet with extensive factories of children's toys; at Tyzabad I saw manufactures in wood, such as bureaus and dressing cases, that would have done credit to any establishment. The mechanics generally sit at their work, using their toes as vises, etc. They are not inventive, but imitative. Their best productions are from European copies. Hindoos are so particular in copying that they should be supplied with a perfect pattern. We heard of a gentleman who gave his native tailor a pair of pantaloons as a pattern, and who found that the new garment was an imitation of the old, even to the patch on the knee, and the rent in another place.

The methods of traveling are not very comfortable. The British have, however, made some fine spacious metaled roads, and shaded them with trees, generally of the tamarind species. The lime used for this purpose is found near the surface. When burning it makes an oxide, with some impurities. In the form of a hydrate

It makes an excellent finishing for houses, inside or outside ; mixed with sand and well pounded it makes a hard and durable cement, so beautiful that it has often been mistaken for marble.

The native roads are poor and narrow, so that traveling by carriage over them is impracticable. Usually the traveling is in light conveyances, borne on the shoulders of men by means of poles. The jampan is like a large chair, with a canvas attachment for the feet, and is carried by two men, relieved when weary by others ; it answers for short distances, and in ascending mountains ; the dandy is similar to it. The palanquin is a covered conveyance of light wood, often ornamented, large enough for a couch, and heavy enough to require four bearers. It has sliding doors at the side, and is the usual carriage of native gentlemen. The dhooley is a less expensive structure of the same size and style, usually covered with colored cotton cloth. The accommodations for travelers are imperfect. The Government has established, on the principal roads, taverns or bungalows, furnished with bedsteads and chairs, and kept by natives who understand European methods of cooking. Here you may either provide or order your own meals, and you are charged according to a fixed scale. Sometimes, however, we find ourselves compelled to cook our meals by the roadside. There are serais for natives. The serai is a tavern built round a court, surrounded by a high wall, and entered by lofty gates, through which the caravans or carts are driven, and which are closed at night-fall. Around the court are rooms where the travelers may rest, and which may be rented for a cent a night; here, too, are to be found shops at which necessaries may be procured, persons who may be employed as cooks; here also are wells, and places of worship.

Sometimes traveling is by elephant. My first ride on this animal was a pleasure excursion at Bareilly. The elephant was driven to the door by the mahout seated on his neck, with an iron instrument having a point to urge the animal forward, and a hook to hold him back. At a signal the elephant went upon his knees, and a ladder having been placed at his back, we mounted and seated ourselves in a houdah, Mr. and Mrs. Thomas on one side, Mrs. Waugh and I on the other. As the animal arose and moved off a chuprasse climbed up his tail and seated himself above it, and we were ready for an aristocratic ride. On we go through the narrow streets of the city, sometimes looking down upon the mud houses, and sometimes trembling lest the elephant should not work his way through without mischief to himself or others. At Lukimpoor we borrowed an elephant of the commissioner to go to Hugauo, fifteen miles distant, where we were to be met with a dhooley to convey us to Seetapore. A crimson pad was placed upon the elephant's back, on which Dr. Butler, brother Gracey, and myself were seated. We started before sunset, and reached Hugauo at midnight. I could not repress the fear that I should roll off and be crushed under the animal's feet. A few days after we received a note from the owner, saying that the elephant had returned without any indication of the burden she had borne. This reminded us too strongly of the fly on the ox.

What has been said shows the facility with which our missionaries may pass from point to point during the season of itinerancy. Each station is provided with a tent and other itinerating requisites. At the suitable period the missionary sending his tent before him on a camel, follows on horseback or in a dhooley, and finds all things in readiness on his arrival. By writing in advance to the Tyceldar he can secure all necessary provisions for his comfort, and facilities for his work.

Within our mission field are various shrines and melas of great veneration and celebrity, such as Hurdwar, Gurmakteser, Bithoor, Ajoodiha, which afford fine opportunities for preaching the Gospel. On our way from Meerut to Bijnour, and from Nugena to Gurmukteser, we found the road thronged with devotees. On arriving at the last place we saw, by estimation, 250,000 people encamped on one side of the stream, and 500,000 on the other. The camps were in regular avenues, watched by a strong police. Here rows of jewelers' shops from Delhi, there rows of toy sellers from Secrora; on this side provisions, on that offerings for the gods. Riding along the lines we stopped at a hollow square of amused spectators, formed round a company of priests who were disfigured with paint, arrayed in saffron robes, and seated cross-legged on the ground, singing the praises of the Ganges in a song, the chorus of which called for *pice*—money—which one of them on his feet stretched out his hand along the lines to receive. On we go to a similar square, within which a dancing girl, bedizened as to her ears, wrists, fingers, nose, and toes, was performing and singing for rewards more freely given than those to the priests. Idols in boats on the water are collecting pice in cloth aprons. In the morning the people bathe in the river, the women at a very early hour, the more devout men next, those less so when the water is warmer; in the evening the Ganges is lighted up with lamps placed in boats, so that it seems a river on fire. The people remain together a week, during which time our missionaries can preach to them. We heard Mr. Hernle, of the Church mission, preach from a wagon on one side of the stream, and Mr. Parker, of our mission at Moradabad, and his assistant, Andreas, on the other. The people listened with attention, often asked questions, and always laughed when the idols were ridiculed. This camp-meeting, attended with so much privation, is for a religious purpose. At the close of the Mela, at the propitious moment of the full moon, of which the priests give the signal, the people together rush into the water to wash away their sins. By these occasions we can reach masses not only from India, but from Thibet and other States north of Hindostan.

Many think of the Hindoos as of the Africans or Indians. The lower classes are indeed ignorant, pressed so hard by poverty that they have little opportunity for culture; and as they move before the stranger without hats or shoes, and with but little covering on other parts of the body, they impress him as a rude and barbarous people. Yet India had a high degree of cultivation in early ages, and her upper classes still exhibit a good degree of learning and refinement. Within our field are three different civilizations. There are none of the Bheels, Ghonds, or other aboriginal tribes. Nearly three-fifths of the population are Hindoos, one-fifth Mohammedan. The Mussulmans, intelligent, enterprising, and occupying the cities in which their ancestors were once the rulers, exert no little influence. The British, though few, exert their power through the magistrates, the laws, and the army.

The vernacular of the Hindoos is Hindee, a soft, beautiful, and flexible language, derived from the Sanscrit. This, though it has long ceased to be a spoken tongue, lies at the foundation of almost every dialect of the East, but is now appropriated to religious records, and, till the Asiatic researches of the English, was shut up for ages in the libraries of the Brahmins.

The language of the Mussulmans is Ordu or Hindustani, derived from the Arabic through the Persian. It is more light and elegant than the Hindee, and better adapted to conversation. The Persian is the learned language of Mohammedans, and the medium of their choicest literature. Many Rajahs have educated Englishmen as tutors in their families, and are themselves acquainted with several tongues of modern Europe. Children of all castes attend the schools of the Government and of the missionaries, which are in all the cities and large towns, and their chief desire is to acquire the English, as it is considered the first qualification for employment, either by the Government or European houses. An illustration of this I found at Gondah, where a negro is employed by the Rajah of Bulrampoor. He was a slave in the United States, escaped to England, embarked in an East Indiaman as a Lascar, remained in Calcutta till he acquired the Hindee, and then went into the service of the Maharajah as a teacher, all his want of qualification being overlooked in his ability to speak English.

The Hindoo literature in the Sanscrit medium consists of poetry, treatises on music, painting, ethics and medicine, systems of philosophy and works on arithmetic, mathematics, astronomy, logic, and law, but nothing to add to our stores of useful knowledge. The literature in the Hindee is very far below this, and that in the Ordu not much above it, though that in Persian is probably an improvement. The Sanscrit literature is confined to the Pundits, and the Persian to the Moonshees, the learned men respectively of the Hindoos and Mohammedans. The whole native literature is full of idle theories, impossible fables, and unsystematized truths. Formerly, in the Government colleges, Persian as well as Sanscrit was taught under the Mogul emperors, and a long time after it was the language of the court and of the law, but Hindustani has taken its place. The change is a wise one. The character of any people depends upon the literature of its leading minds, and this, in turn, upon their language. How different might have been the issue of our rebellion had Spanish been our common medium of thought, or had that tongue even taken the place of the German among us! The political influence coming down upon Hindostan from Western Asia will be less and less. Besides Ordu, Government schools teach Sanscrit, Latin, and Greek, though the last two are elective. Of habits and manners in our field I say little.

The Hindoos are naturally indolent. One of their proverbs is, "If I can ride on horseback, I will not walk; if I can ride in a conveyance, I will not go on horseback; if I can stand, I will not ride; if I can sit, I will not stand; and if I can lie down, I will not sit." Both Hindoos and Mussulmans are polite. At Benares, the Governor-General examining a school asked, "How does the world turn round?" "By your pleasure," was the prompt reply. On leaving the house of a native, the holder said, "I am your servant, what can I do for you?" When I replied, "I ask only your good-will," he bowed down on hands and feet and touched his forehead to the floor. Both Mohammedans and Hindoos listen attentively to preaching, even at the roadside and market-places. Even they who oppose controvert respectfully, and while uttering hard words, and putting searching questions, abstain from personalities, and concede to the missionary both talents and learning. At several points in my journey the head man of the village called to make his salaam. At Bareilly, I said to a native lawyer, who called upon me, "You are the most polite people in the world." "We are obliged to be," he replied; "we are a conquered people." The speech of the masses is highly figurative. To say you lie, their form is, "You say there is no oil in the Til." To express prosperity, "He sits with his five fingers in melted butter." To describe the moderation of the Government, "The cloth is between the iron and the skin." Excessive devotion is "an ass's load of religion." A widow who lost her last child said, "The widow's dove has fled to the bosom of his Savior."

The Hindoos are superstitious. They have countless omens and prognostics. A vulture alighting on the roof of a house, a sneeze, the howl of a jackal in the day-time, the cry of a lizard, the croaking of a raven on the housetop, stepping over a string, pronouncing a monkey's or a miser's name the first thing in the morning, are omens of evil, a lizard falling to the right an omen of good. Plowing, sowing, reaping, are all done with certain ceremonies and on propitious days. Multiplied incantations attend both marriage and death. Each day of the week is devoted to some god, and thought to be connected with some form of good or evil. Sunday is sacred to the sun and to Shiva, and is suitable either for building or sowing seed; Monday to the moon and Mahadeva, and is the time to mount a new horse or set out on a journey; Tuesday, sacred to Mangal, answering to Mars, is the day to fight battles and open forges; Wednesday, sacred to Buddha, corresponding to Mercury, is the day to collect debts and wash clothes; Thursday, sacred to Vrihaspati, is the day for opening a new shop or wearing ornaments; Friday, sacred to Shukra, is when women worship for children lost or on a journey; Saturday, sacred to Shani, answering to Saturn, is the day for acquiring magic, exciting quarrels, and enacting enormities. To a great extent the superstition is hypocrisy. They who arrest the march of armies lest they should destroy insects, build hospitals for disabled animals, and, as Sir James Forbes relates, hire beggars to lie quiet while vermin feast upon them, can shoot, mangle, and cut up their adversaries.

The morals of this region are bad. The Vedants are pantheists, and maintain that God's omnipotence excludes all other power, and his omnipresence all other existence. They deny the immutability of moral distinctions, attribute evil acts to the gods, and think Fakirs may do as they will. The priests teach purification by external means—water, fire, etc.—ascribe efficacy to rites independent of the mind of the worshiper, and think sin may be atoned for by presents to the Brahmins.

Mohammedans seem to ignore immorality of thought. Their prevailing sect is the Sunnites, whose faith has been tinctured with the doctrines of the Shiites through the intercourse between Oude and Persia, and has felt the influence of Paganism, so that its observances in honor of the Imaums, its offerings at the tombs of saints, and the respect it allows to Hindoo divinities very much resemble idolatry, while it has received but little impulse from the reformers. This, perhaps, is not much to be regretted, as the Wahabees themselves are in fundamental error. Maulavee Imail says, "If one alone commits faults equal to all—sinners—yet he shall be pardoned through the blessings of the doctrine of unity." "If he believes this his very sins will be more acceptable than the worship of others." The Hadees, or traditions, the chief guide of Mussulmans, confound moral distinctions. Take the following: There was a holy man who did nothing but righteousness, and a bad one who did nothing but sin. When the latter committed an enormity, the former said to him, "God will punish thee." He replied, "Leave that to God and me." At that moment dying, they came to judgment. God said to the holy man, "Can I save this sinner?" He answered, "Thou art almighty." To this God replied, "Well;" then turning to the bad man he said, "Enter heaven," and to the good, "Go thou into hell."

The practice is like the theory. At Budaon I was told that five at least out of every twenty women are "strange," in the sense of Solomon, and that hundreds of men commit the sin of Sodom; the magistrate said, "Half the men of the city." A man was in jail under sentence of death for killing another under the influence of a boy who stood in the same relation to him that Helen did to Paris. At Seetapore we saw a mosque built by a courtesan with her vicious earnings, and near it an expensive tomb in which her honored remains lie. This is the more remarkable, as Mohammedans do not agree as to the possibility of a woman entering heaven. The houris are *celestial* females, and the faithful who gain paradise are spoken of in the Koran as masculine. At Calcutta the courtesans have petitioned the Governor, setting forth that they perform services connected with the popular religion, and they ask that their rights be protected. Fakirs are consulted as confessors, and often meddle in domestic disputes and lead to the separation of families, while some of the lower class consider it an honor for these holy men to take sinful liberties in their households. The sacred books of the Hindoos limit the learning of females to three things—sweeping the house, cooking food, and ornamenting their persons. Widows can not remarry, and must eat but one meal a day, sleep on the ground, and do the drudgery of the house. Children are often treated with neglect and cruelty, and sometimes repay the unkindness by exposing their parents on the banks of the Ganges. Such are only a few of the enormities practiced here.

Hindoo religion is complicated. There are orthodox and heterodox sects. The former are five—the Shiva, Vishnava, Saura, Sakta, and Ganapatya. In our field, the first and second are the prevailing ones, but their subdivisions and their objects of worship are many, though the most popular are Ram and Krisha. The Vishnavas consider all as heretics who worship other gods than Vishnu, and they avoid all Brahmins who do not belong to them. They adore their god in a series of different forms, as the ministrant ascends the scale of perfection. Their teachers are generally celibates, living in communities, and pursuing a wandering and mendicant life. They have convents, (Maths,) governed by superiors, (Mahants,) and occupied by (Elders) resident disciples.

Initiation in all sects is by whispering in the ear of the disciple a sentence called the "mantra," never to be uttered to profane ears.

The great sacraments of the Hindoos are, 1. The worship of spirits, progenitors, gods, vedas, and men; 2. Obsequial rites; 3. The study of the sacred books; 4. Oblations by fire; 5. Hospitality. There are daily, weekly, monthly, and yearly duties. A Brahmin should divide his day into seven equal parts, and assign to each a religious duty. Usually, however, he spends but four hours a day in devotion. Worship consists in bathing, pouring out drink-offerings to deceased ancestors, repeating certain formulas, making offerings of flowers, water, etc., and uttering, for some time, the name of the guardian god. To facilitate the last operation a rosary of the seeds of either the Tulasi or the Rudrah is used, care being taken that the forefinger shall not touch the beads, for this would render the worshiper unholy. I have one, obtained of a Brahmin through Mr. Jackson. It consists of one hundred and eight beads, on which the name of Ram used to be repeated. Every worshiper is marked after he has made his offering, so that you can see who has paid his daily devotion and before what god. The Vishnavas are marked with white paint. The Ramanujas draw two perpendicular white lines from the root of the hair to the commencement of each eyebrow, a transverse streak across the root of the nose, and a perpendicular line of red in the center; they have also patches on the breast and arm. Some, by means of stamps or cicatrization, impress emblems on their bodies. The subdivision of sects are so numerous that it is said there are 84,000, each founded by a Rishi. Priests are numerous. No particular caste or special qualifications are requisite to either a priest or Fakir, though such as are Brahmins or Celibates are most respected.

Many temples are endowed, but, generally, priests are supported by voluntary contributions; fees on occasion of marriages, births, and deaths; offerings to the manes of the departed; gifts made at the time of worship, and presents offered by pilgrims at the celebrated shrines. The last is a source of great revenue. The Budrinath, alone, is said to receive sixty thousand dollars a year.

The objects of worship are innumerable. India is as full of reverence as the world is of electricity, and worship may be excited in a Hindoo as sparks from a charged and insulated jar. Having no knowledge of the true God, any thing may become god to them, especially if it excite fear, gratitude, or admiration. Some of the Sikhs of the Punjab worship the late General Nicholson, whose heroism made them think him an incarnation. Before his death they built a temple, and set apart a priesthood for him; they did not believe him when he denied that he was a divinity, and they assured him, when he flogged their priests, that they would continue his worship though he killed them.

When the faith of Hindoos was older and purer it inspired art and science. There still remain many monuments of their creative genius, such as the rock temples of the Deccan, and on the island of Salsette. Now that India's religion is degenerated, its science is reduced to proverbs, and its art to mechanical rules. It must be admitted that many of the temples in our field, which are all small, are noteworthy for their proportion, symmetry, and taste, and contain some good specimens of carving, especially in the delineation of animal forms, while the mosques, palaces, and tombs of Lucknow are fine monuments of Saracenic skill; but all these are imitations.

Such, then, is our mission field. It is amply protected by the civil authorities, so that life, limb, and character are as secure as here. It is unoccupied, save only at Tyzabad and Lucknow, by any other missionary society. It is accessible, being just north of the great railway arch which spans the peninsula from Bombay to Calcutta, and traversed with good roads and telegraph lines. It is inhabited by an active and energetic race of men, who, in former ages, have shown a capacity for the highest achievements in philosophy, art, and song, and who are so thickly settled that they may easily be reached in masses. It is healthful. There are regions in which the white men can not long live. Yea, let the line of graves be drawn around the globe, but even then let the Savior's command be heeded. Still we should be grateful and cheerful when Providence calls us to a charming and salubrious land. And India is healthful enough for the temperate and prudent, and beautiful enough for the angels of God.

IX.

VOYAGE TO CHINA.

BEFORE leaving Lucknow I witnessed some feats of jugglery. Performances with snakes, causing the ascent of balls up an inclined plain made of two strings without any agency, the pulling of keys, trinkets, rings, etc., from the mouth of a bystander, the putting a sword down the throat, are the more common feats of the juggler. They none of them struck me as supernatural, though they were all difficult to account for. It is said that the last is done by long practice, which gradually adapts the esophagus to the instrument.

After the Conference was closed the preachers and their wives sat down to a sumptuous repast at the house of brother Messmore. Before the cloth was removed kindly greetings, of which the stranger was to be the bearer, were voted to our missionaries in China, and brother Baume was requested, at the expense of the company, to attend me to Calcutta.

At eight o'clock at night I departed in a ghary, in which was a bed arranged for brother B. and myself. Next morning we arrived at Cawnpore, but being too late for the train we rested for a time at the tavern, and here we heard the gratifying news of Mr. Lincoln's re-election, which produced a shout inside. At 5, P. M., we are off for Calcutta, and at 12 midnight we reach Allahabad, where the train stops until 2, P. M. The trains run at night to avoid the heat of the day. In the leading cities taverns are found, which are conducted in English fashion. Here we stop at Brown's. Stay in hotel, rs. 1.8; breakfast, 1.8; tiffin, hot, 1.8; do., cold, 1.0.0; dinner, 2; board and lodging, per day, rs. 5; chota hazeree, rs. 1; meals, in room, rs. 1 extra; tea, per cup, rs. 0.4.0; coffee, 0.4.0; cherry cordial, pint, rs. 2.8; spirits, per glass, rs. 0.4.0; wines, rs. 0.8.0; soda water, per bottle, 0.4.0; lemonade, rs. 0.6.0; tonic water, rs. 0.8.0; Champagne, rs. 5.8.0; Claret, rs. 3.0.0; Sherry, 3.8.0; brandy, rs. 4.0.0; beer, rs. 1; porter, rs. 1.0.0; Port Wine, rs. 4.0.0; Old Tom, rs. 4.0.0; gin, per square, large, rs. 4.0.0; a carriage and pair per day, rs. 8.0.0; a carriage and horse, rs. 6.0.0; a buggy and horse, rs. 5.0.0; billiards and bagatelle. Surely, a Christian civilized man can find in such a place a supply for all his physical necessities.

At twelve we are off for Calcutta, but it is two o'clock before we reach the station on the other side of the Jumna. At present it is difficult to get freight up and down from the station to the stream. This is done by coolies, who manage to convey the heaviest loads by means of bamboos, and are marched by the officials like a little army.

At Mogul Serai two men, representing themselves as guards of the railroad, and belonging to the Dinapore station, came into our carriage, or car, one of them so drunk that he could not stand. It was said that he had been to court as a witness but was too much intoxicated to testify. Intemperance is very common among the Europeans in India, and the use of intoxicating beverages almost universal. This diminishes the influence of missionaries over the natives.

Riding along, we see large quantities of cotton and rice on the way to market. Men in the elevated fields are gathering the rice crop, others in the lowlands are sowing rice for another season.

At 8 o'clock, P. M., next day, we arrive at Calcutta, where, according to previous arrangement, I put up at Mr. Remfrey's. Mr. R. is a jeweler, who has long resided in India. Mrs. R. is the daughter of the late Rev. Mr. Young, ex-President of the British Conference. She had just returned from England, bringing with her three brides, one for each of the Wesleyan preachers here, and one, a daughter of the "Successful Merchant," for a Mr. Meakins.

On Sabbath morning following, attended the Wesleyan service. Mr. Highfield preached. He is stationed at Barrackpore; his colleague, Mr. Broadbent, resides here, but they exchange. Mr. H. wears the gown and bands, reads the English service, and gives the people a brief discourse from manuscript. I preached in the evening. The imitation of the English Church seemed to me unfortunate. When you invite comparison and do not excel your rival, you fall pitiably low. If men want Episcopalianism they will go to head-quarters for it. There is no room for another Episcopal Church, but there is plenty of room for a downright Methodist one. The Wesleyans here are but beginning. They worship in a hired room, have but a bare dozen of members, and but a few hearers. They have, however, purchased a site for £14,000, and expect to borrow £5,000 of the Missionary Society to put up a building. They receive 200 rupees a month, but pay 130 of it for their hall. The preachers are respectable men, and it is to be hoped that many families, like Mr. Remfrey's, out of respect to the religion of their fathers, will cleave to them.

The Wesleyans have not invaded Northern India, but are confined chiefly to Ceylon, Madras, and the Mysore. In the cool of the evening it is customary to take a walk upon the housetop. Here tea is served, while you stand or sit enjoying a view of the city, and the peculiar orange tinge of an Indian sunset.

The mosquitoes are very troublesome. The temperature is 75 degrees Fahrenheit at midday, and is but little below that in the morning or evening. While here I met with two of the missionaries of the United Presbyterians on their way home from Lahore. Inquiring as to their support I learned that they received, when on duty, 135 rupees a month.

Mr. Broadbent tells me that he has a small congregation of Madras Christians under his care. They worship apart from the whites, but commune with them. The prejudice against color is as great as it is in America. An Englishman would lose caste at once, and probably be disowned by his relatives, if he were to marry a native or even a Eurasian. Not a word was said to me against slavery here, and some disappointment was manifested when I declared against it.

Mr Jacobs, our Consul-General, was kind enough to call and take me out for a ride upon the strand. Mrs. Remfrey invited Dr. Mullens to take tea with me, but he was out of town. The Governor-General invited me to dine with him. He was remarkably pleasant. I gave him an opportunity of discussing the subject of our war by remarking that in the Indian mutiny Americans sympathized with England, but that in the American rebellion England did not reciprocate our sympathy. He replied, "In the beginning of the war Englishmen generally took the part of the North, but in the progress of the struggle they had veered round." When I referred to the election of Mr. Lincoln, and observed that foreign nations had not done him justice, that he was a man of wonderful sagacity, he replied, "Well, if Mr. L. has made some mistakes we should not blame him, for he has not been upon a bed of roses." He maintains that the Sepoy mutiny originated in the offense given to caste by the greased cartridges; caste and religion being identical with the Hindoo. Sir John is evidently a great man, a wise ruler, and a true patriot, and he is universally admired. He should be all this, for his position is one of immense power and influence.

In regard to missions his opinion is that we can do little with the adult population. While multitudes of them have lost faith in their religion, few will apostatize. Our hope is in the children.

December 21st I embarked on the Thunder. She is one of the vessels which the cyclone cast high and dry upon the shore, and she had just been refitted for sea. Being late in getting off we anchor for the night at Garden Reach, within sight of the palace of the late king of Oude. He lives in fine style, and although he receives thirteen lacs of rupees per annum he is half a million in debt. He is exceedingly wasteful, and it is said he has been known to pay £500 for a bird. Our passengers are few; some of them Armenian Christians from the neighborhood of Mt. Ararat, some Jews from Bagdad. Of Armenians, there are said to be 300 families in Calcutta. As we proceed down the bay the north-east monsoon blows, giving us a beam wind, and keeping all passengers from the table but myself. Our sailors are Lascars, and speak Bengali. They lie down, wherever they may be when their time of rest comes, and sleep. It is a singular sight to see servants sleeping by day in the halls, gateways, parks, and even sidewalks of Indian cities, sometimes under a broiling sun. Whenever an Indian has a few moments to spare he spends it in this way.

The navigation of the Hoogly is very dangerous. India has no good harbors but Calcutta, and that can not be approached without a hundred miles of perilous sailing. Pulo Penang and Singapore are excellent harbors, and accessible at all times.

On Sabbath the crew is mustered to see that all are present; they appear neat and clean; some of them are in showy garments. They have but one name apiece, and that is usually short. Several of them had come on board as substitutes for others, and had forgotten the names to which they had originally answered, which caused embarrassment to them and amusement to us. Lascars are fast taking the place of European sailors in these seas; they are obedient, submissive, and cheap. The change is attended with some friction.

A number of European sailors being out of employment at Hong Kong, attacked and destroyed the boarding houses of their Malay rivals. When the police came to produce order, the soldiers re-enforced the disturbers, and a serious row ensued.

The Lascars are very devotional at times, but often sportive. It is amusing to see them washing each other with the hose after the decks are cleaned.

Our crew consists of fifty seamen, thirty-five

firemen, and eight or ten cooks and waiters. The steersmen are from Manilla, the gig men from China, the firemen from Chittagong, the rest from Bengal, except a few from Muscat in Arabia. All are Mussulmans, except the Chinese, who are Buddhists, and the cooks, who are Christians—Catholics. The officers are English.

I preached to the Captain, first and second mates, engineer, and three passengers—about all on board who understood English. I asked the Captain if he had prayers when he had no clergymen. "No," said he, "we so habitually violate Divine Law that it would seem like hypocrisy."

At Christmas dinner we had a cake festooned with flowers, surmounted by an image of Santa Claus, and surrounded by bottles of Champagne and the usual dishes of turkey and plum-pudding. Our vessel is an opium steamer. There are two lines of these steamers running in connection—the one conveying the sales of one month, the other those of the next. We have on board 2,500 chests, each weighing 250 pounds gross. We are to leave forty-two chests at Penang for the local consumption. Opium is produced in India in increasing quantities, and the demand for it is extending over the East. The Government advertises 5,355 chests for sale each month of the year 1865, except December, when the sales are to be 5,362. This is an increase on the sales of 1864, and a great increase on those of 1863. The opium sold at Calcutta is chiefly from the districts of Bahar and Benares, of which the last is generally preferred. Each chest contains a ticket giving an analysis of its contents, and a warrant of them signed by a Government officer. Formerly the price of opium fluctuated much, and there was great gambling in it, but latterly the price has been firmly maintained. It is now worth about $510 a chest, at Hong Kong. Budaon, the seat of one of our missions, is in the opium district. The process of raising it is simple. The capsules of the poppy being cut, the opium oozes out, and is gathered and sold without much preparation. The Government monopolizes the business; it allows no one to raise it without a license. It pays five rupees for two pounds, and sells it at a great advance, thus keeping up the revenue. Many natives have conscience enough to refuse to raise the drug.

These opium vessels bring back, as their return cargo, besides money, English bale goods, spices, camphor, etc.

The coal used by these ships is English. Bengal coal is inferior and bulky. The coal on the island of Labuon is excellent, and yet the company owning it can not compete with the English in the Eastern markets.

A part of our cargo is a flock of sheep. It is said these animals can not be raised at Singapore, though they easily fatten there. The shepherds attending them on shipboard water each with a bottle, which is said to be necessary in order that each may have his portion.

These vessels must be profitable. They get twenty-five rupees for each chest of opium they carry, plus one rupee returned as brokerage. The return cargo also pays well.

And now we are at anchor in Penang, extending from latitude 50 degrees, longitude 100 degrees. It is about fifteen miles long, with an average breadth of twelve miles, with an area of one hundred and sixty square miles. There are perhaps ten thousand acres in fruit-trees, ten thousand in paddy fields, and from seven to ten thousand in spices, nutmegs, cloves, etc. There is a mountain range of granite in the center of the island, with level plains on each side, bordered on the shore with cocoa-nut-trees. The pine and the butter-nut flourish; tin is found in the mountains; its exports of spices, cotton, tobacco, coffee, sugar, and rice amount annually to two or three million dollars. Horned cattle and pigs are raised to advantage here. The seasons scarcely exhibit any change, the thermometer seldom rising above 90 or falling below 80 degrees Fahrenheit at midday. Flowers, and fruits, and fragrance are perennial, and the earth is as beautiful in December as in May. By ascending the hills you get a cooler temperature by ten degrees. Our common vegetables, such as the potato and cabbage, can not be raised. The people would gladly exchange pine-apples for potatoes in equal quantities. A strange disease has overtaken the clove and nutmeg trees, and they are fast dying. The island was purchased by Great Britain of Captain Light, who received it as a marriage portion with his wife, the daughter of the king of Queda, and here is a British fort with a regiment of Sepoys. Georgetown, the port, is the capital and seat of government of the strait's settlement. It contains a population of 2,200. The island, with a strip on the main land opposite, of which the English have the sovereignty, contains about 100,000. The British, though the rulers, are few. The original inhabitants are Malays, but since the island fell under British rule Hindostanese, Burmese, Siamese, and above all, Chinese, have entered in. The last are generally merchants, manufacturers, and mechanics. They frequently marry into Malay families, and from this union the more industrious and honest citizens arise. The Malays form the lowest stratum of society, the Chinese the highest, the Indian the middle class. The last are usually coolies from Madras, who are attracted by high wages—thirteen cents a day—and after laying up money usually return to India to enjoy it. The European population, though small, consists of representatives from many nations, English, Dutch, Portuguese, and French. The Malay language is the *Lingua Franca* of the East. It is soft and to a great extent monosyllabic. The people are fond of figures of speech; thus, the sun is the eye of day, the police officer, the man of eyes. The Catholics have here a bishop, a cathedral, and a number of priests, some of whom spend their lives in self-denying labors in the jungle, and of course make progress among the people. I was told that the Church of England minister is of the Colenso school. The London Missionary Society had a station here, but upon the opening of China they abandoned it. Germans occupied the abandoned station until death carried them off. The premises are now in the hands of Mr. Chapman, of Bristol, who, with Mr. Grant, is preaching and carrying on an orphanage on Mr. Müller's plan. Thus far, he says, the Lord has sustained him.

He professes to be of no sect, though he evidently sympathizes with the Plymouth brethren. Mr. Bain, our consul at Penang, was very polite, and took me to his house for dinner. Here, on the 29th of December, we have peas and asparagus with our meats, water-melons and plantains with our dessert.

The Armenian Church is very powerful, widely extended, and greatly influential. It is found in all the great cities of Asia Minor, Egypt, India, China, and the eastern islands. Its members are generally merchants, and are often men of wealth, talents, and enterprise. They are not Protestant, though they are separated from the Greek Church in consequence of the accidental absence of their Bishop from the Council of Chalcedon, whose decrees they never received. A majority of the Church, as early as the sixth century, adopted monophysite views. They insert four apocryphal books among their canonical; namely, the history of Joseph and Asenath, and the Testament of the Twelve Patriarchs, which they add to the Old Testament, and the Epistle of the Corinthians to St. Paul, and the third Epistle of Paul to the Corinthians to the New.

With some of the Armenians on board we have free conversation. They say their creed differs in nothing essential from that of the

Greek Church. When asked why they do not return to it, they reply, "We have no means of preserving our nationality but by our religion and language." They claim that the country originally extending from the east side of the Euphrates to the Koordistan Mountains, was the primitive seat of the human race, and that their language was that of Adam, and they bring many arguments for this opinion. They say their people embraced Christianity under the labors of St. Bartholomew and St. Thaddeus of the apostolic college. They, after having suffered a gradual religious declension, in the year 318 religion was revived among them under the labors of an apostle of their own, St. Gregory. Armenians now claim three millions, of whom perhaps ten thousand are scattered abroad, the rest are in their primitive seats, Georgia, Persia, and Armenia. Like the Poles, they are partitioned between three great empires, the Russian, Persian, and Turkish. They are somewhat superstitious, and lay great stress upon the fasts of Wednesday and Friday. They are governed ecclesiastically by a Patriarch. The Patriarch appoints the Archbishops—one at Jerusalem and one at Constantinople—as well as the bishops and the prelates of Julpha, who control the Armenian Churches of the East. At that place is a college of priests. These are sent out to the Churches of Bombay, Calcutta, Penang, Singapore, Batavia, etc. They go without their families, and remain five years, when they return to their homes and others are sent out in their places. Although the Churches have no voice in the selection of their pastors they are well pleased with the itinerancy. As the compensation in their Churches is unequal an effort is made to equalize by sending a clergyman whose last appointment was poor to a good one, and *vice versa.* In two instances, namely, at Penang and Calcutta, this itinerancy was recently interfered with, but in both cases, the interference being injurious, was abandoned and regretted. The Church at Penang consists of only one family, Mr. Anthony's, and pays fifty rupees a month besides furnishing house and servant for the priest. The Church at Batavia is rich; hence, formerly, the priest sent to Penang after remaining at Penang three years was sent to Batavia to spend the remaining two years of his term. The Church of Calcutta being rich a pastor solicited and obtained a permanent settlement, but, growing proud and arrogant, insulted his superior and was excommunicated. The compensation allowed the priests of Calcutta is 2,400 rupees a year, $1,200 each. They reside in the church, and are three in number. The Armenians are liberal. The Church at Calcutta, for instance, disburses 400 rupees a month to the poor from property received by will. They often endow their churches. As we entered Singapore it rained so copiously as to interfere with our view of its magnificent harbor. The shores of the mainland and the beautiful islands, both those off the coast of Sumatra and those to the south of Singapore, are charming. They do not experience the droughts from which England suffers, but enjoy frequent rains, so that their surface all the year round is like an English lawn in Spring.

Going on shore I called upon Mr. Stone, the American consul, who gave me a note to Rev. Mr. Keasbury. Getting into a cab I drove through the city, which has an appearance of bustle and thrift; the Chinese being both merchants and mechanics; the stores and the shops of the artisans were side by side; the barbers were at work out-of-doors; the cocks were crowing in the stores, and pigs were exposed for sale in baskets. The surface of the country, its hedgerows, its trees, and its gardens were beautifully green. Many of the coolies were seen at work, naked from the umbilicus upward and from the thighs downward. The Madrasses, or Klings, as they are called, are the boatmen and the most industrious of the laborers. They have a dislike to their rivals, the Chinese, which gives rise to frequent rows between them.

Mr. Keasbury was one of the missionaries of the London Missionary Society. When it ordered its forces here to China he determined to remain, and for fifteen years he has been laboring on his own account, sustained by local subscriptions. I judge, however, that Protestantism has nothing of importance here. New-Year's on shipboard was ushered in by ringing the bells, shouting, laughing, frolicking, which commencing on the quarter-deck was soon removed to the main deck and afterward the forecastle. The passengers had all left; the rain descended in torrents; the ship took in freight all day, although it was Sabbath; it was too inclement to be on deck, too dark to read, and there was no one to converse with; the rain coming through the sky-light drove me to my state-room.

The Christians have some good churches in Singapore, nor are they altogether inactive. The Ladies' Bible Society distributes a large number of Bibles and tracts, but their operations, although extended over the Indian Ocean from Borneo to Ceylon, and from Bàli to Siam, and embracing English, Spanish, Portuguese, Dutch, Tamil, Malay, Hindostani, Teloogoo, and Boogese beneficiaries, do not cost over $1,300 a year.

Now near the equator, the north star is out of sight, the southern cross in view. We are off. The wind is high and contrary; the white waves dash against the shores of Sumatra, Malacca, and especially Bintang and the reef of rocks extending from it to the light-house. The rain pours down. My boots being so wet that I could not get them on I borrowed a pair of the captain and ventured on deck when the rain relaxed, but, having left my port-hole open, when I returned I found my bed, bedding, books, hat-box, and trunk saturated. Day after day might be written rough, rougher, roughest. The "Thunder" bears up nobly against the monsoon. The waves roll over the quarter-deck; one can take no exercise; the ports being closed the air of the cabin is impure; the ship is filled, even the state-rooms, with opium, fish, and melted ghee, part of which is rancid. The small-pox appears among the sailors, and the sick man, in order to prevent the spread of the disease, was brought into the cabin and placed in a state-room near mine; we have no physician on board; the thermometer stands steadily at 85 degrees Fahrenheit. On we go through the Palawan Pass, with shoals and breakers on both sides. Now and then we see the sun, but the clouds return after the rain. At length the storm seems to do its worst. The jib-boom is carried away; the figure-head is dashed to pieces; the cry of a man overboard pierces our ears; the frightened Lascars cry Allah! allah! and throw a life-preserver, but the man misses it; the captain runs astern, and with encouraging words throws a rope; at the lucky moment when the ship lurches the sailor seizes it and is saved. A moment more he had been lost; for no boat could have lived a minute in the sea.

Passing the Royal Charlotte Shoals the sea abated, but a ring around the moon portended a renewal of the storm.

On Sabbath we had service in the cabin by my urgent solicitation. A few officers of the boat attended.

Now we are in the Palawan Straits, with shoals on each side of us. Three sailors are on the yards of the foremast all day, looking out for breakers, and we frequently stop for soundings. My head, which was bruised against the guards, and my arm, which was skinned against my berth, begin to feel better.

We carry cannon as a protection against pirates, who are partly Chinese and partly Malays. The northern coast of Borneo is a great resort for them. Sir James Brooke's settlement at Saranac has done great service in putting them down. He keeps a gun-boat, which sails to Singapore semi-monthly, and which sometimes pursues depredators, though it receives no reward for its service. On one of these occasions, we are told, the Bishop of Labuan was on board and did good execution with his rifle. These pirates usually sell their native prisoners into slavery, but kill their British. The British Government should take Sir James Brooke's settlement under its protection.

We have probably made a mistake in sailing by the Pass; we could hardly have had worse weather by the direct route, which would have been five hundred miles shorter.

Four more sailors fall sick. The sailor and blacksmith are extemporizing a jib-boom. The storm having abated we set the spanker and trisail to steady the ship. Now we are in sight of Mandaro and several other of the Philippine islands.

The captain one evening, having caught one of his Lascars smoking opium, captures his pipe, lamp box, etc., and notifies him that he can not allow the practice, because it renders the men useless, subjects the ship to great expense; for when the stock of opium gives out the smokers can be kept alive only by expensive medicines, such as camphor, and exposes the smokers to great temptation, especially when in loading or unloading a chest is broken and the balls spilled.

As we get near to Manilla we have a clear day and a glorious sunset.

Long confinement, bad air, resulting from the cargo and the sick room, and depression of spirits began to take away my appetite and disorder my system. The table, at the same time, grew less inviting; the red ants were in the bread; they crept out of the rice, the sugar, the nuts; they crawled over the plates and the cloth, the floors and the berths.

Now we are abreast Manilla. We coast the Island of Luzon nearly all day, charmed with the beautiful shores, the green and luxurious vegetation, and the hills in the distance.

Having passed the island the storm rages afresh. Sails are torn, crockery broken, rain, wind, horrors on horrors, darkness, thick darkness! Next day storm continues without abatement. Toward noon tripsail and topsail are up but reefed, and the wind is bearing us at eleven knots an hour, and promises to bring us to port at 4, P. M. But now the wind veers and the storm increases. Four o'clock comes and no land in sight; five o'clock, and no land; six, and no land. We spend the night outside the harbor waiting for the day. Morning comes and by nine o'clock we are ready to land. I was the only passenger. As I stepped into the Chinese boat all alone the coolies got into a quarrel over me, and accidentally threw me down and hurt me, but not seriously. I could not remonstrate, for I knew not Chinese, and could only use my cane. Having landed I cried out "Oriental," and was soon piloted thither; coolies carrying my luggage behind me. Calling for a room I was shown into a narrow apartment without furniture, save a bed, table, and chair. It had a hole for a window near the ceiling and eight small panes of glass, equal to about two of our common ones. I called for chicken broth, but what was brought me was more like brine than broth. I sent for a physician, but his prescription was unfortunate. The mail was to go to Foo Chow at eight o'clock, but I was unable to go. Wrote to Mr. Conger, American Consul, but he had gone to Macao. As a last resort dropped a line to Rev. Dr. Legge, who kindly called and took me to his house. Next day being Sabbath, went to church and heard Dr. Legge in the morning. He announced me for the night, but I was unable to fill the appointment. Dr. Kane was called in to see me, and pronounced that I was sinking from fatigue and want of nourishment. Next day went in a chair to the Consulate, the public gardens, the terraces overlooking the harbor, and returned fatigued but better. In a few days, under the good management of Dr. Kane and the kind treatment of Dr. Legge's excellent Christian family, I was able to start for Foo Chow by the Undine. I did not leave until I had called upon the chaplain, Dr. Irvine, a jaunt of four miles, and taken a general survey of the city. Bishop Smith, of the English Church, has gone home discouraged. He was a weak man; for he refused to serve as Vice-President of an Asiatic Society because it put Dr. Legge upon a par with him. Some years since the chaplaincy of Victoria was exchanged for a parish in Hampshire. The Hampshire incumbent, being uncomfortable, was glad to get safely out of England, while the colonial chaplain, having got tired of the East, would have been glad to get back without a parish, and doubly glad to get back with one. There was no power to unsettle the arrangement after it had received the sanction of Government.

The missions here are, first, Dr. Legge's. It has one hundred members, many of them in good circumstances, and three preaching places; second, the Church Mission, which has fifty members; third, the German or Basle Missions, say thirty members; fourth, the Roman Catholic Mission, which is not doing much.

It was a painful thing to land sick in this great empire without a knowledge of the language and without a single friend. Mr. Piercy, of the Wesleyan Mission, came to China without knowing any man in the empire except one who was dead when he landed, and without having any resources of his own to draw upon, or any Missionary Society to sustain him. He was a local preacher, who visited China from a sort of impulse within which he could not resist. Dr. Legge kindly took him to his home, where he was overjoyed with his reception. He worked for his living, learned the Chinese language, and as soon as he could converse in it began his missionary labors. A crazy man in England wrote to him that he would sustain him, and that as an earnest of what he would do he had deposited to his credit £100 with the Wesleyan Missionary Society, for which he could draw. He showed the letter to a banker, who took his check and cashed it. When the draft with Mr. Piercy's letter arrived the Society inquired into the circumstances, and were so well pleased with the result that they paid the draft and adopted Mr. P. as their missionary. He is now superintendent of the missions in Canton.

It is delightful to find a friend in a foreign land. I can not express the gratitude I feel to Dr. Legge. By all the missions I was kindly received, but by none so kindly as by those of the London Missionary Society. Their missionaries seem to be men of large heart, large culture, broad views, and catholic feelings, and their wives admirable specimens of exalted Christian womanhood.

During my stay at Hong Kong I met Dr. Kerr of the American Mission at Canton, Mr. Kongar, the American Consul at Hong Kong, Mr. Jones, American Consul at Macao, Dr. Eastlake, the Principal of St. Paul's College, and the missionaries of the Church Mission.

In my walks about the city I called at the Catholic Cathedral, and found in connection with it, 1. An English school numbering forty-five scholars, some of them Eurasians; 2. A Portuguese school, not so large; 3. A Chinese school, in which are ten young men training for the priesthood. The Cathedral is plain and spacious. It contains a marble arch which was presented by Victor Emmanuel. My next point was Miss Baxter's school. She has about thirty boys and as many girls, and is sustained partly by fees and partly by donations. Next, the Orphan Asylum. sustained by the ladies of Berlin. They have thirty infants in care, one of which has lost both feet by frost. Near by is a Diocesan school, in a building of imposing appearance, though it has not done much yet.

From thence we proceeded to St. Paul's College; a fine building, the front of which was intended for the Bishop's palace. They have a small class, say of sixteen or twenty boys, whom they are teaching English in hope to employ them in the ministry; but they complain that as soon as the youth get acquainted with the English language they go into secular business as clerks, etc. The Catholics have the advantage over the English Church in this respect; they teach their young pupils Latin only, which is of no use to them in secular business. The Germans have a similar advantage.

The English Mission only claims forty Chinese communicants.

Now we are off for Foo Chow. The boat is a beauty, the captain a gentleman. Next day we arrive at Double Island. Here Mr. Johnston, a missionary from Maine, resides. He occupies very good premises. His wife teaches a boarding-school, which is independent, and is supported, in part, by the labors of the girls. When Mr. J. first entered upon duty, in 1848, he found the prejudice against foreigners intense; arising from the coolie slave-trade, of which this island was the seat. But the influence of this is gradually subsiding. He has baptized forty since he arrived, and thinks his prospect fair. He is, however, about to remove his location, as the foreigners have deserted the island and gone to Swatow, and the natives are following them, so that the island will soon be nearly deserted. There is here a small temple of polished granite, admirably carved in *alto relievo.* It is to the goddess of Mercy, or Queen of Heaven, and reminds one of Mariolatry and the resemblance between Buddhism and Romanism.

On we go to Swatow, where we remain some time. It is a poor-looking place, on a low strip of land with here and there a green spot, but beyond that, presenting the appearance which the whole coast does of cold granite. Swatow contains about 20,000 inhabitants, a small number of whom are Europeans, who, however, are increasing. The custom-house officers are British. Mr. Hart has the general superintendence of them. Baron Meriton, a Frenchman, is collector at Foo Chow. January 1st we arrived at Amoy, in the neighborhood of which was an insurgent force, that caused much uneasiness. We were all day discharging cargo, the most valuable of which was opium, though there was grain of various kinds, chiefly different species of pulse. Here is a mission superintended by Mr. Stronach. The shipping in the harbor is nearly all junks, attractive by their gaudy decorations in anticipation of New-Year, which in China begins the twenty-sixth of the month, January, and remarkable for the cannon they carry, which is said to be a necessary defense against pirates in these waters. The foreign shipping is mostly English—not an American flag to be seen. Much of the shipping is damaged, probably by the typhoon.

Next day we are off, and on the following morning we are approaching the mouth of the Min. It was Sabbath, and I proposed preaching, but we could not get more than three or four together, and as the captain could not lèave the deck because the navigation was dangerous, he deemed it best to decline. The perilous approach to the Min is a serious drawback to the commerce of Foo Chow. Now we are in the tortuous stream. Foo Chow is about forty miles up. When within twelve miles, at Pagoda Island, we come to anchor. The hills on each side of the river look cold and barren, yet they are terraced to the top, and in Summer present an appearance of luxuriant vegetation. The cultivation is mostly by hand. The irrigation is sometimes artificial; sometimes by springs in the mountain-sides.

Here and there is a tomb cut out of the granite. A boat belonging to Russel & Co. came alongside to convey me to the city. Eleven oarsmen strike their oars into the blue waters, but soon they drop them with a shout. A favoring breeze had arisen, and filling the yellow sails it soon brought us to our wharf. Obtaining a chair we passed through a crowded street, very narrow and paved with stone. Merchants were very busy on each side, and appeared to have a great variety of business. Suddenly, turning under an arch, we rise by a long flight of stone steps to the house of Mr. Maclay. The family were absent, but in a few minutes came home from church.

Weary, wan, ghost-like, 20,000 miles and more from home, the sight of an American, a brother, a minister was almost too much for me. I was at home. Here was brother Maclay, as kind as a natural brother could be, and Mrs. Maclay, as considerate as a sister or a mother; here was a fireside where the Bible was read, and happy Christian children joined in the songs of Zion. It was an overcoming joy, and the silent tears stole down my wan cheeks as I sat back in my chair and leaned my head against the wall.

X.

OUR CHINA MISSION.

IN this chapter I propose to give a view of our China Mission as I found it in the year 1865, touching missionaries, mission property, location, and general prospects of usefulness.

The mission force is as follows: Rev. Mr. Maclay and wife, Mr. and Mrs. Gibson, Mr. and Mrs. Baldwin, Mr. and Mrs. Sites, and the Misses Woolston. The latter are sisters in charge of the girls' orphanage; sensible, neat, devout, well educated, and thoroughly devoted to their work. Mr. Sites is a man of imposing appearance, good attainments, ardent piety, strong attachments to the Church, and full consecration to his mission. He exceeds the expectations of his friends in the facility with which he acquires the Chinese language, and the influence he exerts over the people. Mr. Baldwin is scholarly, and has a mind keen, rapid, well fitted for the literary labor of the mission. Mr. Gibson is an able missionary, and it is greatly to be regretted that the failing health of his wife should render it necessary for him to return. Mr. Maclay, the superintendent, is worthy of his place. He has a quick, well-educated, and well-disciplined mind, and to habits of business and a heart for his work, he joins correct judgment and a strong will. Yet, with his great firmness he has great kindness, and he avoids all parade of authority. Careful investigation proves his administration to have been judicious throughout. Of the happy wives—now in health and in the prime of life—of these good men, I need only say, May God long preserve them to his Church! One brother, (Martin,) who was active in the mission when I started to it, was in his grave when I arrived. The cholera carried him off, and one of his children with him. His widow was in the mission, inquiring what was God's will concerning her, and had just concluded before I left to return to the United States. The last words of brother Martin were, "Tell my friends at home that it pays to be religious."

It will be a satisfaction to the Church to know that our missionaries are comfortably situated. They have good houses and furniture, and are amply supplied with the necessaries and comforts of life. The number of servants usually employed by a missionary in China is five; namely, cook, waiter, cooly for rough work, washerman, and nurse. Each receives $3.50 per month and boards himself.

There is in the city, besides the missionaries, a considerable Christian society, consisting of a number of English, French, and American officials and merchants, and several very respectable physicians.

The native force in our mission last year was as follows:

NATIVE HELPERS.—Hu Iong Mi, Tang Ieu K'ong, Hu Po Mi, Li Iu Mi, Ling Ching Ting, Li Tai Sing, Yeh Ing Kwang, Li Seng Mi, Hu Sing Mi, Ngu Siu Mi, Hu Hieng Mi, Li Cha Mi.

CHAPEL KEEPERS.—Li Taik Ong, Ting Neng Seng, Ung Sing La, Ting Neng Taik, Sie Chai Mi, Ung Sieu Mi, Wong Heng T'ung, Ngok Hing Liong, Wong Taik Kwong.

SCHOOL TEACHERS.—Wong T'ai Hung, Ling Kie Ping, Ting K'aik K'ung, Tang K'eng Ming, Ting Ka Ch'ung, Sie Chung Chung.

The work, for the present, is divided into circuits as follows:

I. Nantai circuit, with three appointments; namely, Tienang Tong, in the southern part of the city of Foo Chow, and two out-stations; namely, Changlok and Yeuping. At the first brother Hu Po Mi has been laboring. The latter is a prefectural city, where we have been seeking to gain an entrance, though under much opposition and difficulty.

II. South Ta Chau circuit, with the following appointments: Ching Sing Ting, (in the city,) Lien Kong, (a neighboring city where native helpers have been employed,) Mingan, (a city between the other two, which is occasionally visited, and where books and tracts are distributed as opportunity offers.)

III. North Foo Chow circuit, containing East-street Church, in the city, and no other appointment, although the missionary organized a class at Tien Iong, twenty-five miles distant, and visited, in company with brother Sites and some other native helpers, the district cities of Kucheng, Long Wong, and many other places new to Protestant missionaries.

IV. Western circuit, consisting of Ngukang, Yeh Iong, and other adjacent places. The missionary has been very enterprising, making excursions with native helpers, preaching and distributing books and tracts, and has opened a new place of preaching; namely, Minchiang.

V. South Nantai circuit, consisting of Sieu Liang, in the suburbs of Foo Chow, and the Hokch'ang district, south of the city. In both places a chapel is found.

The plan of the work for the year was as follows:

1. EAST FOO CHOW CIRCUIT, comprising the Min and Changlok districts: S. L. Baldwin, Missionary; Tang Ieu K'ong, Hu Iong Mi, Hu Sing Mi, native helpers.

2. NANTAI CIRCUIT, comprising Hokch'ang and Ingkok districts, O. Gibson, Missionary; Yeh Ing Kwang, Ling Ching Ting, native helpers.

3. NORTH FOO CHOW CIRCUIT, comprising Long Wong and Lien Kong districts: R. S. Maclay, Missionary; Hu Po Mi, Ngu Siu Mi, Li Tai Sing, native helpers.

4. WESTERN CIRCUIT, comprising Aukwang and Min-ch'iang districts: Nathan Sites, Missionary; Li Iu Mi, Li Seng Mi, Li Cha Mi, native helpers.

5. INTERIOR CIRCUIT, comprising the Kuch'eng and Pingnang districts: missionary to be supplied; Hu Hieng Mi, native helper.

6. BOYS' BOARDING-SCHOOL—Otis Gibson, Principal.

7. GIRLS' BOARDING-SCHOOL—Miss Beulah Woolston, Preceptress; Miss S. H. Woolston, Assistant.

8. PRINTING-OFFICE—S. L. Baldwin, Superintendent.

9. TRANSLATING COMMITTEE—R. S. Maclay, Otis Gibson.

10. FOUNDLING ASYLUM—Mrs. H. C. Maclay.

11. AMERICAN SUNDAY-SCHOOL—Mrs. Ettie E. Baldwin.

We have begun our literary labors auspiciously. A colloquial New Testament has been published, with a colored map of Palestine, and a list of the miracles, parables, and discourses of Christ. A revised edition will soon appear. The work has been adopted by all the Protestant missions in the city, and it has been translated chiefly by our own missionaries, assisted by those of the Presbyterian Board. Dr. Maclay has prepared an English and Chinese dictionary in the Foo Chow dialect, alphabetically arranged. Our Discipline has been printed during the year, and also the Methodist Hymn-Book, a small arithmetic by brother Gibson, and a monthly record.

The expenses of the office for the year were $1,379.90. The receipts were, from the American Bible Society, $966.41; American Board of Missions, $133.27; for English printing, from mercantile community, $450.65. Besides numerous copies of the Methodist Catechism, General Rules and Ritual, and minor matters, our printing-office issued during the year of

I. Scriptures.	Copies.	Pages.
Colloquial Matthew,	4,000	208,000
Classical "	6,000	252,000
Reference "	500	40,000
Gospels and Acts,	500	158,000
Galatians and Hebrews,	2,500	170,000
James to Revelation,	2,500	135,000
Colloquial New Testament,	1,500	669,000
Printed for American Board of Missions portions of New Testament,	3,500	173,000
Total of Scriptures,	21,000	1,805,000
II. Tracts, Scientific Books, etc.	Copies.	Pages.
Ten Commandments,	13,550	133,500
Hymn-books,	1,825	90,100
Gibson's Arithmetic,	500	21,000
C. C. Baldwin's Catechism,	150	19,500

In all, 2,071,100 pages.

Besides the mission force already described, we have a Christian boarding-school teacher, and six hands in the printing-office, all Christian. We have a boarding-school with twelve boys, another with twenty-three girls. The property belonging to the mission consists of,

1. A printing-office, worth $5,000; 2. The mission compound, on a healthy, eligible spot overlooking the city of Foo Chow. It contains six lots, each being 150 feet by 100. On this are six dwelling-houses, all except two of brick, with stone foundations, and valued as follows: Number one, $600; number two, $600; number three, $1,500; number four, $1,500; number five, $3,000; number six, $5,000. There are three church edifices valued as follows; namely: One in the city, $2,500; one on the north side of the river, $2,500; one on the south side of the river, $3,000; all brick. At Ato a small chapel, on rented land, worth $250. Nine chapels at out-stations, all rented but two, one at Ngukang, valued at $500; one at Kinchang, valued at $250. A chapel at Quaninchang, $50. An orphanage for castaway children, valued at $600. The number of children in it was thirty-one, and they were supported by local contributions. As to the sphere of operation, on week-days our congregations are composed of all classes, on Sabbath of

members and other serious persons. There are five preaching-places in the city, and an average attendance on Sabbath—including pupils and servants—of fifty persons at each place. Beyond the city we have six Sunday congregations, with an average attendance of fifteen at each. The number of communicants is 131; of probationers, 28; of baptisms during past year, 51; and of additions, 34. The Sunday-schools are eight, and their scholars 150. The amount contributed by the members for missionary purposes, $55. The probable number of Pagans to whom we preach weekly is 3,000; namely, 2,000 within the city and 1,000 without. Our members are generally intelligent and pious Christians. About fifty of them are dependent, more or less, upon the mission for support.

The location of our mission is healthful and beautiful. The country in the valley of the Min is mountainous. In our evening walks we pass down the mountain on the east side of the city. It is covered with graves. I thought at first they were hewn out of the granite, but, upon examination, found that they are made of Chunam. On the way we come to a set of graves belonging to the royal family of the Loo Choo islands. They are showy; and in the midst of them is a monument expressing the imperial will that the ground should be thus appropriated. There is much intercourse between the Loo Choo islands and Foo Chow, which contains a Loo Choo quarter. When the officers come over to pay their annual tribute, they generally leave their subordinates here while they go to Pekin. These very frequently engage in trade while waiting. Foo Chow has also much intercourse with Formosa, which is only sixty or eighty miles from the mouth of the Min, and which is an important granary for this prefecture. The stranger, in walking upon the hills, is struck with the number of vaults, or houses in which coffins awaiting interment are found. The doors are usually open. There is no effluvia from these, for the coffins, though usually of wood, are so cemented and varnished as to be air-tight. People often go to great expense at a funeral. It sometimes happens that when death occurs the family do not feel able to endure the expense of interment. In that case they send the coffin to a waiting-hall, or, perhaps, conclude to keep it in the house, until they obtain means for the funeral. Thousands do the latter, sometimes using the inclosure of the corpse for a settee.

At marriage, also, the Chinese go to great expense, often impoverishing themselves at a wedding.

It is painful to see the poor Chinese women hobbling along on their little feet. But custom reconciles all things. Women here are generally betrothed in their infancy, often with the specific understanding that their feet shall be crippled.

The public roads are all narrow—four feet wide—as if made for foot-passengers. If the emperor were to come from Pekin to Foo Chow, he must come by palanquin. The rivers are used as far as may be, and the boats are generally drawn by men on the banks, by means of ropes. When they come to a rapid in the stream, they wait until forty or fifty have collected, when they join and draw the boats over, one by one.

In my evening walk on the day before New-Year's I saw a fight. A young man knocked an old one down, and was beating him severely, when some coolies bearing a palanquin dropped their burden, seized the stronger combatant, and handled him roughly, saying, "You must not beat an old man." His reply was, "He owes me. This is the last day of the year. If I do not collect my debt to-day it will be canceled." New-Year's is the only Sabbath of the Chinese. Then all business is suspended, all respectable people gather their families and friends for feasting, and the streets are abandoned to beggars and gamblers. The law against gambling is by custom suspended for twenty days after New-Year's, and during all this period groups of gamblers may be seen at every corner.

The hill-sides are generally cultivated wherever there are no graves, and in the valleys is luxuriant vegetation. The fields are cultivated, not mined. What we call agriculture is usually mining. We take all out of the soil and put nothing back, leaving it so much poorer than before as the crop is worth. Not so in China. The fields, which need no fences, so closely are they watched, are daily enriched by the offal of the city, which is carried in buckets on the shoulders of men to be spread over their surface. The city needs no drains. All its garbage and offerings to Cloacina are sold and carried off day by day; but the stranger needs a handkerchief well perfumed to hold his nose in his evening walks afield.

The city is the capital of Fokien, one of the five ports thrown open to the British by the treaty of 1842, and contains seven hundred thousand inhabitants. It stands on a plain on both sides of the Min, but the old city is on the left bank, defended by a wall of ten miles circuit, thirty feet high and twelve thick, which has towers at short intervals, that look gay with flags and bear the marks of activity, as the city is threatened by a rebel force said to be very strong and intrenched near Swatow. The entrance is by seven gates commanded by towers. A bridge, four hundred and twenty paces long, resting on an island in the stream, and supported by forty-nine stout piers, crosses the river, and connects the two parts of the city. Foo Chow has fine residences for the civil and military authorities, and large granaries. It is celebrated for the manufacture of porcelain, and is said to contain hundreds of furnaces. It has also factories for cloth and cotton goods. Lead mines are near by, but its trade, which is supposed to amount to seven or eight millions, is its chief support. The streets are very narrow, not more than twelve feet from house to house. A fire having occurred in the main street, the Government ordered that it should be widened three feet. The stores are built of wood, and touch each other, so that if one in a block gives way the rest follow. A block of fifty houses fell down a few days since. The fronts are movable, so that there is no need of doors. When the shop is closed it presents to the street a wooden wall, and when it is opened this is taken down. The chief security against fire consists of large tanks of water in the street above ground. Another arrangement is a number of fire-proof walls by which the houses are separated. Usually, when a fire begins and can not be at once subdued, it is allowed to advance until it is arrested by one of these walls. The houses are low, and the roofs project over the street to form a protection against the sun, which almost shuts out its light.

There are numerous remarkable wells just outside the city wall, all more or less mineral, and some strong of sulphur. They differ very much in temperature, some being 104 degrees Fahrenheit; one 140 degrees. The Catholics say they first taught the Chinese the use of them. Bath-houses are constructed all around them. In these you may have an ordinary bath for four cents, and a swimming bath for twenty cents. You may also have refreshments to order. It is somewhat disgusting to a European to see the bathers going from their baths in a state of nudity to the refreshment apartment, and returning to the baths again after having partaken. The poor people bathe in the springs in the open air. A dozen may sometimes be seen in one spring. Their only expense is a cash or two, that is, a mill or two, which is given to the boys who watch their clothes. The waters are supposed to be especially valuable in cutaneous diseases, which are common in China.

The population of the city is not homogeneous. There is a Tartar garrison, where daily rations are distributed to two thousand soldiers. The population of the Tartar quarter is said to exceed twenty thousand. Besides soldiers and their families, there must be some engaged in other pursuits. There is a mosque in the city, quite inferior, however. The worshipers are chiefly Mongols, of whom there are about thirty families.

But it is time we took a particular look at our churches. Brother Gibson takes me in a chair to a chapel on the right side of the river, where services are held three times a week besides Sabbath. It is probably well located to catch strangers, but is a small, dirty, forbidding room, kept by an old man, whose son, as we entered, lay in the aisle unconscious, having taken too much opium, probably with a view to kill himself. The old man offered me his pipe filled and lighted, but on my declining he applied it to his own lips. It was in the shape of a cane, and of the same length. Returning we called at a large temple, which presented nothing elegant, either in architecture or decorations, and seemed to have a large space for a worshiping congregation. The gods are various and infamous, and incense was burning on every altar.

Another day we go to see a church in the city proper. Down successive flights of stone steps to a tnronged street, along this—which runs parallel with the river—for some distance, then turning north, we cross the stone bridge to the island; through the island, which is thickly populated; then over another stone bridge to the city proper. After traveling some three miles through a crowd we reach the city wall, and pass through gates and massive arches to the interior. About a mile from the south gate of the city is our church, called East-Street Church. It is a plain, neat structure, with a parsonage in the rear, and stands on the spot where, a year ago, there was a mob which tore down the buildings we formerly occupied, and abused the women and children. After repeated applications for redress we got an indemnity sufficient to build our new house, but the Government was too weak to bring the offenders to justice. A native helper, one of the Hu family, lives in the parsonage. As soon as the doors were open for worship the people began to enter, one with a basket of live poultry, another with vegetables, another with a string of money, or cash, round his neck. They took seats, and some remained to the close; but many arose and departed after hearing a short time, their places, in some instances, being supplied by fresh comers, so that at the termination of the meeting we still had a good congregation. After a short prayer a sermon was delivered, and then I made an address, which the missionary interpreted. In the vestibule tea was prepared for the preachers. It is said that on any day, during business hours, you may have a crowd by opening the doors. Curiosity brings them in. One aged man, after service, asked for and received a copy of the Chinese Bible. On Sabbath, in the church on the mission compound, we had Chinese service in the morning. Yeh Ing preached. He is one of our native helpers, and apparently a man of power, culture, and piety. After his discourse I addressed the assembly through an interpreter.

In the afternoon I preached in English. There were present, besides the members of our mission, some persons from the Presbyterian, and other Europcans, the American Consul, etc. Mrs. Baldwin played the melodeon. In the evening the missionaries assembled in Mr. Maclay's parlor for prayer and sacred song, thus closing the holy day delightfully, and in a way to remind us of home, sweet home. During the next week I had the happiness to attend a monthly meeting of the missionaries, in which their bills are audited. These bills are for native helpers and incidental charges. They are announced, explained, and, if no objection be made, allowed and recorded.

On February 1st I went with Mr. Sites to his residence, Ngu Kang. This is up the river some distance. For the purpose of communicating with the mission he hires a boat at $16 a month. The boatmen own it. Once the mission owned a boat, and these boatmen worked it. Some of the native Christians wished to manage it, and were of course preferred, but being unskillful they soon lost it. This boat resembles the flat-boats of the Mississippi, and is remarkably neat. It is said that the boats in China are among the neatest things in it. Many of them, like this, are occupied by families. The head man of this boat lives in it. He has a wife and child, and the former takes her place at the oar with other rowers. We go part way by oars, then the boatmen get out and draw the boat by ropes, as a canal-boat. When the wind favors sails are used.

After landing we had a three-mile journey to reach the mission residence, which contains a chapel in the center. One each side is a little village, the one entirely Pagan, the other partly Christian. Our cause here gained rapidly for a time, but now the line is sharply drawn between the Pagan and the Christian community, and the opposing forces are hostile.

We next go to the Peach Farm, "To Cheng;" here there is a chapel. Near by is a large house, in which several Christians dwell. The houses of the peasantry are usually wooden, and of great length and uniform style. I was in several of their parlors or audience rooms. They were open-roofed, supported by large wooden columns, without any floor but the earth, and without any furniture but a table and some rude benches. In one I saw a plow and a rake, and in another a hen sitting in a basket. This region is mountainous, but here and there the valleys open into rich plains. In these wheat is growing, which I am told will be followed during the season by two crops of rice. On the hill-sides, on terraces, potatoes and many other vegetables are raised. An acre in the valley is said to be worth $300.

Before leaving Ngu Kang the Christians were assembled in their church; they represented five different classes. After the usual religious services brother Sites gave the people an opportunity of speaking, and interpreted their addresses to me. They abounded in thanks for my visit, prayers for my safe return, desires that I would ask the prayers of American Christians for China, and that Chinese Christians might stand fast in the Lord, and solicitations that I would bear these salutations to my country. Sia Seh desires, above all things, that the Bishop should ask the American Church to pray that Chinese Christians may be filled with the Spirit, and that converting power may come down upon the nation.

Li Moi Sing, a sister sixty-four years old, prays that Christians on both sides of the globe may be of one mind and heart. She has unutterable joy in Christ.

Li Anna, a sister seventy-four years old, says she has great peace in believing, .thanks the grace of the Father and the Son that she meets a Bishop, and prays that he may safely reach his home on earth, and finally his home in heaven, where she expects to meet him again.

I closed the meeting with an address and prayer. In due time I returned to Foo Chow. Our land journey is performed in chairs; it is over a path concerning which there are many legends of robbers in the olden time. Our voyage down the river is nine miles, and we make but three miles an hour, as the tide is against us.

Next day I visited Miss Woolston's school. The furniture is plain, rough, and cheap, but clean; the children are plainly but neatly dressed.

There are benches for chairs, mattresses for beds, and bamboo frames for pillows. All this is that they may not be discontented on returning home. Misses Woolston are much encouraged by accessions recently received. There are now twenty-three girls under instruction.

One of the first objects of my attention was Mr. Gibson's school, the scholars of which, thirteen in number, had been dismissed for the New-Year's holidays. The boys are generally Christians.

One day we had in our city church a sort of reception. All our members were collected, with the members of other missions and all the missionaries of the American Board, except Mr. Baldwin, who was sick. After singing and prayer, and reading the Scriptures, I made an address, or sermon, brother Maclay interpreting. Then the brethren spoke voluntarily, each delivering a short address. They spoke with remarkable readiness, earnestness, and grace. Their words were reported to me and translated by the superintendent, but they are too voluminous to be inserted here. They were full of gratitude to the American Church, of compliments to her representative, and prayers for God's cause in both America and China, and for the universal coming of Christ's kingdom.

On the succeeding Sabbath we had quarterly-meeting in the church on the mission compound—Tien Ang Tong. Brother Gibson held a love-feast at half-past nine, A. M., which continued till near twelve. Tea and cake were distributed instead of bread and water. Brother G. alluded to his departure, and intimated that it might be his last service. Mr. Baldwin favored me with an abstract of the speaking. Dr. Maclay preached at twelve on the Eighth Commandment, one of a series on the Decalogue. He writes his discourses, but studies them well. At two o'clock I preached in the same church to an English congregation.

My next visit was to the church under the care of Mr. Baldwin—Ching Sing Tong. It is a substantial brick building. In the vestry we found Hu Sing Mi, who visited the United States in company with Dr. Wentworth, and found a home for two years in the family of J. Stephenson, Esq., New York City. His room contained many conveniences; such as, cooking stove, iron bedstead, and bedding, of American manufacture, all, I understand, presented to him by his kind benefactor in America. Also, portraits of Messrs. Stephenson, Odell, and other well-known faces. A local preacher—Tang Ien Kong—lives in the parsonage adjoining the church. The bell having been rung, the people came in from the street and took seats, not so many as usual, in consequence of New-Year's. The local preacher preached. I followed with a brief address, which seemed to interest them. Mr. Baldwin interpreted for me.

CONTROVERSY.

Harmony prevails among the mission with the exception of a dispute about certain terms.

Two hundred years ago a controversy arose in the Roman Catholic Church in China concerning the proper name for God; the Jesuits using the term Shangti, the Dominicans Shin. The matter was referred to the Pope, who compromised by adopting a new term, Teen Chu, Heavenly Lord. The first Protestant missionaries used Shin for God and Hung for Spirit. Dr. Medhurst advocated the use of Shangti for God and Shin for Spirit. About the year 1846 those who used Shin for God adopted Ling for Spirit. The Protestant missionaries are now divided into two parties, about equal in number. In 1847 the missions in Foo Chow adopted Shin and Hung, often using Shangti as an appellative; subsequently they adopted Shin and Ling. This continued until 1860. About this time the Church of England used Shangti and Shin, and in the following year all the missionaries of the American Board here adopted the same terms. In August, 1865, a majority of our mission being in favor of them, waived their preference, and adopted, on Mr. Gibson's motion, the following, after some months of consideration:

"WHEREAS, The members of this mission are divided in opinion as to the best terms to be used in China for God and Spirit, and also with reference to the best version of the Scriptures in Chinese; therefore,

"*Resolved*, That the several members of the mission, and the native helpers in our employ, should, for the present, use the Chinese terms they severally prefer for God and the Spirit, and also the version of the Scriptures which they deem best."

At that time the mission stood, three for Shangti and Shin, two for Shin and Ling. Among the Protestant missionaries of Foo Chow the vote stood, eight in favor of Shangti and Shin, two in favor of Shin and Ling. Our native helpers stood, eight in favor of Shangti and Shin, one in favor of Shin and Ling. All the native helpers of other missions were in favor of Shangti and Shin. There was a prospect that under this compromise resolution harmony might be secured; but it seems that the minority, as they studied the question, found it magnifying in importance, ceasing to be a philological question, and becoming a moral one. Not content with the liberty to use the terms they preferred, they felt bound to contend with those who used others. One would not allow his native helpers to use them, withdrew his members from the monthly concert, and kept his scholars from our public meetings. Two refused to circulate the version of the Scriptures preferred by the mission—distributing that of Drs. Bridgman and Culbertson—and all books in which the objectionable terms occur, and could not allow to be sung in their churches the hymns in which they are employed. One of these has returned, the other remains; but, no doubt, time will cure the discord. I must confess that after hearing the whole question discussed, I could but look upon the difference as of but little consequence, though the controversy may be very evil in its results if it should be continued.

OTHER MISSIONS.

There are in Foo Chow the following missions besides our own: 1. The missions of the American Board. They have four missionaries, with their wives; namely, L. B. Peet, C. C. Baldwin, Charles Hartwell, and S. F. Woodin. The

Church of England Mission has two missionaries, with their wives; namely, J. R. Wolfe and A. W. Cribb. The premises of the American Board are partly within and partly without the city wall.

Calling upon the missionaries of the American Board, I found they had just purchased an eligible piece of property for $3,400. On one occasion I dined with Mr. Baldwin—whose wife has an interesting school, to which she seems devoted—and on another occasion with Mr. Peet. I also called upon Mr. Wolfe, Church Missionary, by whom I was kindly received. His house is on an eminence commanding a fine view of the city, in which stand prominently both the Catholic and Episcopal churches, substantial, ornamental, and admirably located. The former is very large, and its architecture, arrangements, and ornaments are all in Chinese taste. It has a garden and a nunnery attached to it, and a foundling hospital opposite. It claims to have three thousand members.

The missionaries of the different Protestant missions come together in a monthly concert of prayer. I led the meeting on one of these occasions, opening it with an address. These brethren seem to regard each other as members of one body, and work together in harmony.

ENCOURAGEMENTS.

The following sources of encouragement may be noted: 1. The decline of prejudices against foreigners and against the Gospel; 2. The removal of all legal obstructions to the spread of Christianity among the people, and to its propagation throughout the country; 3. A steady increase of the influence of Christian nations in China; 4. Legal protection for both native and foreign Christians; 5. The readiness of the people to receive missionaries, and the invitations from them in various parts; 6. Proofs of conversion and the power of the Gospel in the lives of Chinese Christians; 7. Gifts, graces, and usefulness of our native helpers. They are well-formed, well-dressed, noble-looking men. One of them, of the celebrated family of Hu, told me he was stationed one hundred miles off, in a sickly place. Sometimes he gets the ague and comes back to recruit, but is soon at his post again.

BUDDHIST MONASTERY.

Before leaving Foo Chow I went to the celebrated Buddhist monastery at Kushan Mountain. We descend the river in the mission boat about six miles. Then landing, we take a chair and ascend the mountain, up which a broad stone pavement leads all the way to the monastery. There are rest-houses on the way, where refreshments may be obtained. The mountain is rocky and sterile, though a few pine-trees are making slow progress here and there, where the soil allows them to take root. The views of the river, and city, and surrounding country from the different rest-houses are charming. As we approach the monastery we see a number of disabled cattle, which are in charge of a herdsman, and which, it is said, are preserved from death and suffering by the monks, who deem it a high virtue to preserve life. There are springs near the monastery, and the water is received in a large tank, which seems filled with fishes. The building is in a very concealed but romantic spot. Though only one story, it covers a large space. The images at the entrance are colossal. We were just in time to see the monks assemble for worship; they are said to be seventy in number. They are of various ages; all have their heads shaved, are clad in yellow robes, and look melancholy. The worship consists of genuflections, recitations from their sacred books in Pali, which few, if any, understand, singing, etc. The exercises are regulated by bells, though time is kept by beat of drum. In passing through the library a priest politely insisted on our taking tea, and heartily rejected money that was offered for it. A short time since there was a devotee locked up in a cell for meditation and purification, but having served out the time of his vow he had passed out.

The camphor-tree spreads its ample shadows over this sacred spot, and the tea-plant grows on the hills around. The location is so cool and healthful that our brethren resort to it as a sanitarium. They have a contract with the monks, by which certain rooms shall always be ready for them at a dollar a week each. The missionaries furnish them, and provide their own meals; but how revolting to take a family to such a place, making them familiar with the forms of idolatry! It is like hiring a spot in the suburbs of hell in which to pass the cold weather.

EXPERIENCE OF NATIVE HELPERS.

My coming to Foo Chow excited much curiosity and conversation, not merely among the missions but beyond. My visit and my relations became generally known through the members of the Church and the servants of the households of the missionaries. As I was passing, with brother Maclay, a group of heathen Chinese, one of them said, "There goes the Bishop. He is like Jesus Christ; he goes round the world preaching the Gospel." This shows that the common people know something of Christ, and the nature and scope of his religion.

Before I departed the missionaries assembled, and delivered to me in writing a grateful and affectionate address, signed by all their number, to which I replied as best I could. The chief members of the mission favored me with their autographs, and preceded them with remarks which the superintendent translated. The substance of some of these remarks I give. Yek Ing Kuang says: "Entering the Christian Church I had two thoughts; namely, Christ died for me and for the sins of the world. My nation is given up to idolatry. Your face is as the face of an angel. Pray for me."

Hu Po Mi said: "I rejoice in your visit to Foo Chow, because it is a proof that the Western nations are constrained by the love of Christ to love us who live in the East. Before seeing your face I seemed to be with you in the Gospel. Ten thousand thanks to you and the Churches of America."

Li Ju Mi says: "My heart rejoices when I read, 'He that believeth shall be saved,' and sorrows when I read, 'He that believeth not shall be damned.' I have seen believers enjoy great peace and die in the Lord. We are three brothers, but the youngest, King Sing, twenty-four years old, died last year, ninth moon, twenty-seventh day. He had great peace, and in departing said, 'My sins are great, but my Savior is sufficient. To go home is better than to stay. Be diligent in preaching, for Christ only can save.'"

Sia Seh Ong, native exhorter, said: "Thanks to the Heavenly for the joy of seeing your face. Pen can not record the fullness of grace I have in my inmost soul. May you return in safety, and cease not to pray that God may pour out his Holy Spirit upon us that China may be saved!"

Trong Tai Hung says: "I believe in Jesus. Neither is there salvation in any other."

Hu Hieng Mi says: "As to my entering the Church, see John v, 24; viii, 51; iii, 18."

Trong Keng Chung says: "A great blessing to observe the love which the Bishop has shown in leaving his country, home, and kindred, to endure the sufferings of a long voyage, and meet the perils of travel in strange lands, to encourage feeble Christians in trying to serve God. I thank him for his exhortation to filial piety and brotherly love. My salutations to the Christian Churches of America."

Lai Tai Sing says: "Seeing the Bishop, and hearing his words, I rejoice. Salutations to the Churches in the United States. From you we have received the Gospel missionaries, who crossed the ocean to preach the Word of Life and establish Christian schools. In Mr. Gibson's school I received instructions, and the Holy Spirit opened my heart to receive the Savior. Pray that I may be a useful disciple."

Le Sing Mi says: "Joy and gladness that I behold thee. Thou hast received the love of Christ to bear thee over oceans to meet here the disciples of the Lord. God grant thee great peace of soul in returning to thine own house! Greet the elders and the brethren for me."

Ting Ka Chung and son say: "Coming to Ngu Kang, and seeing the face of the Bishop, my soul is filled with joy. The Heavenly Father hath brought thee to China to encourage his holy Church."

The Koi Hung class of fourteen members write: "Through the grace of the Savior we see you. God grant you grace and a peaceful return! Greet the American Church, and pray for China."

Tang Yeu Keong says: "When I beheld the Bishop's face my heart greatly rejoiced. When I saw his feebleness, and considered that it was for Christ's sake he suffered, that he might cross the wide oceans to come for God's people, and that he did not fear the discomforts and dangers of the voyage, only desiring to aid the few sheep in these ends of the earth, truly, my heart is lost in wonder and love. I thus know you to be a genuine Bishop. See John x, 11. Your visit and your example will be a great blessing to us all. May God abundantly bless you, and bring you to the end of your voyage in peace!"

Nu Sin Mi says: "Through God's grace I know to travel in the way to heaven. In my heart I love you with the love of Christ. God grant you a prosperous voyage! Though parted from you in body, we shall still pray for you and your family, and the whole Church of God in America. We heartily thank you all for sending us the Gospel and a messenger to strengthen us in the faith of Christ."

Sing Ching Ting writes: "My salutations. With regard to my sins, see 1 Tim. i, 15. As to my darkness, see Matt. iv, 16. As to my light, see 1 John iv, 10; John iii, 16; Romans viii, 32. As to Christian love, it is shown in the labors and sufferings of the missionaries and their Bishop, enabling us who were dead to live in Christ. Now, seeing the Bishop's face, we rejoice with exceeding joy. I love the Bishop, the missionaries, with their wives and children, as my own brothers and sisters. China is given up to idolatry. Pray for us! Grace, mercy, and peace be with you all!"

Hu Yong Mi writes: "Peace and myriads of blessings upon the Bishop! Thanks to God, who hath given you a prosperous journey. Seeing your face reminds me of the joy of Joseph when he beheld the face of his father, Jacob; but I am unworthy of the comparison. Forgive this boldness. Unceasing thanks to the Triune God, who hath saved sinners. The joy is unspeakable. Your eye hath seen the fellowship of saints. You have not shrunk from peril that you might increase our knowledge and joy. Having received such favor, I beg you accept the thanks of one less than the least of all saints. May God evermore be merciful to you! You have told us to bear the cross. My soul answers, 'Thy cross, Lord, will I bear.' We send out the Macedonian cry. Pray for us. Paul desired the Thessalonians to pray for him. Be pleased, also, to convey our salutations to the bishops, pastors, and members of the Church in the United States."

I make the quotations without embarrassment, because, though they are no compliment to me personally, they show the feeling of our Chinese brethren toward the Church at home.

www.ingramcontent.com/pod-product-compliance
Lightning Source LLC
LaVergne TN
LVHW010235110826
845151LV00004B/1299
9781425525026